PLAY WITH THEM— THERAPLAY GROUPS IN THE CLASSROOM

ABOUT THE AUTHORS

PHYLLIS RUBIN received her M.A. in Speech/Language Therapy from DePaul University, Chicago, and holds a certificate as a Theraplay therapist. She is a speech/language therapist for the Proviso Area for Exceptional Children, Maywood, Illinois. She has worked with children from preschool through junior high school age who are developmentally delayed, educably and trainably mentally handicapped, autistic, learning disabled, emotionally disturbed, as well as speech/language disordered. Rubin has given many presentations on Theraplay and Theraplay Groups to both national and local professional associations. She is presently pursuing a doctoral degree in clinical psychology.

JEANINE TREGAY received her M.Ed. degree in special education from National College of Education, Evanston, Illinois. She also has a background in social services. She has worked with early childhood, learning disabilities, behavior disorders, and developmentally disabled populations in public and private schools, and in residential facilities. She has been co-presenter with Rubin at national and local professional conventions. Presently, she is pursuing a doctoral degree in special education.

PLAY WITH THEM–

THERAPLAY GROUPS
IN THE CLASSROOM
A Technique for Professionals
Who Work with Children

By

PHYLLIS B. RUBIN

and

JEANINE TREGAY

With a Contribution by

Mary Alice DaCosse

With a Foreword by

Ann M. Jernberg, Ph.D.

Clinical Director of The Theraplay Institute
Chicago, Illinois
Author of "Theraplay"

C H A R L E S   C   T H O M A S   •   P U B L I S H E R
Springfield • Illinois • U.S.A.

Published and Distributed Throughout the World by

CHARLES C THOMAS • PUBLISHER
2600 South First Street
Springfield, Illinois 62794-9265

© *1989 by* CHARLES C THOMAS • PUBLISHER
ISBN 0-398-05579-3 (cloth)
ISBN 0-398-06715-5 (paper)
Library of Congress Catalog Card Number: 89-4730

Printed in the United States of America
SC-R-3

Library of Congress Cataloging-in-Publication Data

Rubin, Phyllis B.
    Play with them—theraplay groups in the classroom : a technique
for professionals who work with children / by Phyllis B. Rubin and
Jeanine L. Tregay ; with a contribution by Mary Alice DaCosse ; with
a foreword by Ann M. Jernberg.
        p.   cm.
    Bibliography: p.
    Includes index.
    ISBN 0-398-05579-3 — ISBN 0-398-06715-5 (pbk.)
    1. Special education.   2. Play therapy.   I. Tregay, Jeanine L.
II. DaCosse, Mary Alice.   III. Title.
    [DNLM: 1. Education, Special.   2. Play Therapy—in infancy &
childhood.   WS 350.2 R896P]
LC3969.R83   1989
371.9—dc19
DNLM/DLC
for Library of Congress   89-4730
                                                                        CIP

To Our Families

FOREWORD

I am so grateful to Phyllis Rubin and Jeanine Tregay, not only for giving me the honor of writing the foreword to this wonderful book, but for having the wisdom, spunk and generosity to write it in the first place. They have exceeded what I could have envisioned in writing my own book, *Theraplay,* ten years ago. Their message comes at a time when too many children grow up doubting both their own self-worth and the emotional investment that adults are willing (or able) to make in them. The authors have demonstrated that the Theraplay method can be applied to the classroom to give children hope, joy, and the conviction that there are adults who care about them as genuinely valuable human beings. Rubin and Tregay convincingly guide teachers through the steps that will help vast numbers of normal and not-so-normal children develop self-confidence, joie de vivre, and the assurance that the world can be a trustworthy and enjoyable place after all. Their gift of this book to teachers and their students is what I mean by generosity.

Rubin and Tregay's contributions are twofold. First they present helpful principles and then they tell the reader specifically how to apply them. Some of these principles would be startling in their novelty, and perhaps even unacceptable to some individuals, were they not offered with respect and compassion. Readers will find themselves feeling grateful, curious and excited to try out many of the book's suggestions. "Unlearning or How to Stop Teaching" (in Chapter 5) is one such example. The repeated elucidation of the Rules for Group Theraplay (NO HURTS— STICK TOGETHER—HAVE FUN) is another.

Their introductory descriptions of Theraplay Groups in action are intriguing and joyful. The Pretend Face Painting as it would be viewed through the eyes of an outside observer (Chapter 1) is particularly noteworthy.

Throughout their book, in beautiful style and with lovely examples, they direct specific suggestions to leaders of child Theraplay Groups. Their focus is on helping both individual members and the group as a whole. The experience they provide the reader is lively, personal, and action-oriented. Thus, even in their language they carry out Theraplay's directly engaging approach.

Rubin and Tregay's book could well have been entitled "Enhancing Humane Behavior: Lessons in Respect and Empathy." Just as the teachers themselves are taught with respect and empathy, so also is that same attitude conveyed to the children. The readers will learn to attend to and communicate a child's special, invaluable individuality. At the same time they will learn how to acknowledge children's fears, anxieties, anger and sadness. They will learn how to encourage children to share their small hurts and major traumas. And they will learn how to help them share their triumphs. They will learn how to recognize the new trust that grows when children begin to feel safe in sharing with adults and with one another. And, since most of their sharing will happen in a loving, upbeat climate, they will learn to feel hope and joy in the process.

In sum, I am convinced that the labors of Rubin and Tregay and the usefulness of *Play With Them: Theraplay Groups in the Classroom* will be deeply appreciated not only by the children themselves but by those many individuals who will interact with them in their future.

Ann M. Jernberg, Ph.D.

INTRODUCTION

Y ou are about to read a book that would be better in video! The technique of Theraplay that guides our thinking throughout this book is one that is highly visual and non-verbal. We struggled in the beginning, not knowing how to put into words an experience, a feeling, an atmosphere. What we came up with was a combination of discussion, narratives of actual group sessions, and stories that might evoke in you the feelings similar to those that must be present in a Theraplay Group.

It is important that you "feel" our groups. That you feel how intimate they are; how regressive and nurturing they can be. That you feel the unconditional acceptance. And that you feel the playfulness. Groups based on Theraplay are all of these.

Theraplay Groups are for children who have emotional needs: children who are withdrawn (or "quiet"), over-active (or "bossy"), frightened (or "shy"), compulsive, or rigid, for example. Children with learning problems, speech and language problems, intellectual deficits, academic problems, and/or family problems often have unmet emotional needs and can benefit from a Theraplay Group.

Theraplay Groups are adult-directed structured play groups in which all the participants, the adult included, are actively involved together in pleasant, fun activities. These games are geared to foster self-esteem, a sense of belonging, the ability to care for oneself and for others, and to develop increased trust of others. The members of a Theraplay Group often are able to provide for each other what they may not be able to get otherwise: nurturing, attention, recognition, and appreciation.

Theraplay has a unique characteristic that you will notice immediately: it is highly nurturing, so much so that frequently the activities we use can look "babyish." It is not unusual to play a lotion or powder game, or to feed each other in a Theraplay Group. As you go through this book, you will learn why we do these things.

We used Theraplay Groups in the classroom to create a sense of family and connectedness among a group of people who spent a great deal of time together. This technique can be used in other types of settings as well, such as hospitals, preschools, day care centers, or mental health centers.

Theraplay Groups are for professionals who work with children. Teachers, special educators, psychologists, social workers, counselors, speech/language therapists, all might find this approach useful in their settings and within their repertoires. In this book, we speak directly to those in schools. Those of you in other settings can adapt the technique to your needs.

In writing this book, we considered the issue of non-sexist language. We took the following points into account. Our style and content required that we clearly differentiate between the adults and children described in the book. The book is based on our experience working primarily with female adults and male children. Presently, most primary caretakers are mothers, most professionals who work with young children are women, and most children in special education are male. We might wish this were different, but it is not. Thus, for the sake of simplicity and ease of reading, our writing reflects this reality. Do not interpret this to mean that Theraplay is a "women's" approach to working with children. Both men and women therapists use Theraplay. Neither are we saying that Theraplay and Theraplay Groups are for only troubled boys, because this is certainly not the case.

We have ourselves come a long way in writing this book. It all started almost ten years ago. Susan Riley was the senior Theraplay therapist, and Phyllis Rubin the junior Theraplay therapist, for the Proviso Area for Exceptional Children cooperative in Maywood, Illinois. (Both Riley and Rubin were also speech/language therapists.) At the end of one school year, Riley began leading a Theraplay Group in a classroom and told Rubin about it, suggesting that Rubin might want to try to do the same the next year.

Rubin did not really want to, however. She could not envision herself successfully leading **a group** of special education children. But, somehow, she was compelled, and found the courage, to try. She had been working individually with a very withdrawn child in a behavior disorders class. In hopes that a group may serve to transition the child from individual, to group, to appropriate classroom functioning, Rubin asked the classroom teacher if she would like to try a Theraplay Group in her room. The teacher was willing.

They began a successful group, a successful teacher/Group leader relationship, and modified the group as they went along. They shared their knowledge and learned from each other. And they learned from the Group.

During that same year, Rubin was providing individual Theraplay for a child in Jeanine Tregay's behavior disorders class. Tregay was concerned about three other children in her class and was planning to refer them for individual Theraplay. When Tregay told Rubin about these three children, Rubin said she could not possibly see them all. But Rubin suggested a Theraplay Group. Thinking a group might help the timid, withdrawn child she was seeing for individual Theraplay, Rubin saw this as the rationale for the group.

Tregay was interested, but she had other ideas for this group. It would not be for just the Theraplay child, but for **everyone.** This way, her three other children, and the whole class, would be the focus of the group. Hopefully, everyone could get a little bit of Theraplay, which by now, she was convinced was a good thing.

Rubin led the group for three years, until she was no longer able to set aside time for leading groups. She was, however, able to set aside time to support teachers who wanted to learn how to lead the groups themselves. Would Tregay like to learn? No! Well then, Rubin could not lead the group. But Tregay wanted the group to continue in her room. Finally, she agreed, with trepidation, to try it herself with supervision and support. She took the Introductory Workshop in Theraplay, given by The Theraplay Institute, and she began videotaping her groups for supervision with Rubin after school.

Then one day, Tregay said that these groups were so beneficial, Rubin should write about them. Rubin said she would if Tregay would help her! And here we are.

ACKNOWLEDGMENTS

First and foremost, we wish to thank Dr. Ann Jernberg, creator of the Theraplay technique and clinical director of The Theraplay Institute. She continuously encouraged our efforts, supported and promoted the Theraplay Group training program, and gave us invaluable editing advice on the book. Her trust in us and her belief in the value of Theraplay Groups in the classroom was an inspiration from start to finish.

The following people supported us as we developed the Theraplay Group approach, made presentations, and actualized the Theraplay Group training program. From the Proviso Area for Exceptional Children, Maywood, Illinois: Larry Foster, Richard Perry, Susan Riley, Terry Smith, and Debbi Greengold Welch. From District 87, Berkeley, Illinois: Richard Riley and Neil Winebrenner. From The Theraplay Institute: Adrienne Allert and Phyllis Booth.

Leonard Grossman, Sonja Hall, Naomi Hene Diamond, and Helen Rubin were kind enough to edit and proof-read our manuscript. The various perspectives with which they viewed our writing helped make the book more readable for people in a wide range of professions. Pauline Coffman and Ruth Schmitt provided additional advice. Naomi Diamond deserves special thanks for suggesting the title for the book.

We especially wish to thank the eight people who participated in our first Theraplay Group training program. They are: Betty Brown, Mary Alice DaCosse, Aviva Goldman, Karen McCabe, Susan Noble Pelafas, Karen Schuster, Lisa Tatar, and Ellen Whelan. The experiences they shared, and our experience working with them had a significant impact on the book. Their willingness to try something new, and their enthusiasm about their Theraplay Groups brought us new insights from the viewpoint of the trainee (i.e., the readers of this book).

Without a computer, and someone to save us from power outages, this book would have been lost many times over. We wonder whether we would ever have written this without the assistance and support of

Howard Rubin. He not only provided computer expertise and editing advice, but took an active interest in our project, spent countless hours helping us with it, and really cared that it come to fruition. We cannot thank him enough.

Phyllis Rubin
Jeanine Tregay

CONTENTS

PLAY WITH THEM— THERAPLAY GROUPS IN THE CLASSROOM

Chapter 1

WHAT IS A THERAPLAY GROUP?

You are visiting a school. You are stopping in the classrooms for brief glimpses of school life. You are in for some surprises.

The first room is a pre-school special education class. The children, their teacher, and the group leader are all on the floor, in a circle, on their stomachs, facing into the circle. The leader is holding a cotton ball and putting it down on the floor in front of her. She says: "I'm gonna blow it to Jamie." She blows the ball with a big Whoosh all the way across the middle of the circle to Jamie. Everybody laughs. Then Jamie blows the ball. But the leader stops him, "Wait a minute! Wait a minute! Who you gonna blow it to?" (Jamie forgot to "announce" the recipient of the cotton ball.) Jamie says: "Miss Walsh." (He has picked his teacher.) Leader: "OK. Blow!" Jamie blows, but the ball only goes half way across the circle, and Jamie does not pursue it. Leader: "Come on. Blow it more." Jamie moves up to the ball and blows again, blowing it all the way to Miss Walsh. Leader: "Good! Who are you gonna blow it to, Miss Walsh?"

Miss Walsh: "I'm gonna blow it to Mannie. Ready? Here it comes! (She takes a deep and exaggerated breath) Ah-ah-ah- Whoosh!" Once again, the ball only goes half way, and the leader steps in to encourage the teacher: "Come on, get it, get it!" Miss Walsh moves up to the ball, gives a big blow, and sends the ball right to Mannie's face. Everybody laughs.

The leader then turns to Mannie and says: "Mannie, who are you gonna blow it to?" But Mannie only points. Leader: "What's his name?" Mannie mumbles a name. Leader: "Nicholas? OK. Give it a blow." But Mannie, who forever looks sad and out of it, aloof and on the edge of the group, does not blow. Instead, he throws the cotton ball across the circle. The kids laugh. But the adults do not reprimand. They stay pleasant. The leader retrieves the ball, puts it in front of Mannie, and, with a smile, says: "Wait a minute. No fair throwing! Mannie! (Getting his attention.) Mannie! A blow—blow it. Can you blow?" Mannie blows the

3

ball. Leader: "Good! More, more!" And Mannie blows it again, this time almost all the way across the circle. Leader: "Good! Good for you!"

What fun they are having! You wonder what they might be learning from that activity. But they are only pre-schoolers. Pre-school classes always use play. And they are special education children at that.

So you move down the hall to a regular kindergarten room. But the entire class is on the floor here also, barely able to fit on the rug! The teacher, leading her own group, is starting a game. She has a large paint brush in her hand. "Guess what we're going to do today. We're going to paint our faces! Bet you never did that before. I'll show you how. In this carton I have some special colors. I have magical green, magical purple, magical blue. You can't see them, but something special will happen when I start painting. Teddy, get ready, cause I'm going to paint your face." She puts the clean brush into an empty egg carton. "First, I'm going to paint your wonderful nose blue." She takes the clean brush out of the carton and strokes it gently and artistically over Teddy's nose. "Ooo! Oh, how beautiful! And your eyebrows. I'll make them magical silver." Again she dips the brush into the empty carton, then stroking Teddy's brows in admiration. "And your chin with that special dimple. Here's some magical red for the hole in your dimple." "Pop!" She dabs some pretend red on Teddy's chin. "Look, everybody. Doesn't he look wonderful?" And Teddy grins as everyone Ooo's and Ah's. "Now Teddy, you get to do Sharon's face." Teddy takes the paint brush and turns to Sharon. "I like your ears best. I'm going to paint them magical yellow with green and purple stripes." And he does. You are amazed at how fascinated the children are by this activity. With gazes fixed on each other, they are watching the painting unfold as if it were really happening. The **atmosphere** is magical — captivating. It almost makes you remember what it felt like to be a child!

Reluctantly, you leave this class and go on to another special education room of children six to eight years old. Since these children are school-age, you are sure they will be doing typical schoolwork at desks. But no, they too are on the floor in a circle, the teacher and aide with them, all smiles. You are soon to find out that they are passing around silly faces. The teacher says: "Oh, I've got one! (And facing the child next to her, she crosses her eyes and twists her nose with her fingers.) Everyone laughs including the teacher, proud that she surprised everyone with a funny face. Smiling, Sam says: "I can't do that. I can't cross eyes." But he does it anyway. And the first funny face gets passed around the circle. Leader: "Oh! Look at Ann's face!" More laughter at each person's turn. "Oh! Look at Tim! Does he pass along a good face!" They are having such fun! You wonder what this all means, why it is being done, and how the teachers justify all this play in school. Meanwhile, you move on.

The next class is a regular first grade with thirty children. Now you are not so surprised when you find them on the floor also. But they are not in a circle. They are on their hands and knees, one in back of the other, each one holding onto the feet of the child in front, making a long snake. And that is just what they are playing. Slowly and carefully, they wind around the room. The teacher who is watching and directing says, "OK, now the snake is going to sleep. Be careful when you go to sleep so no one gets hurt." And the kids lean over carefully and lie down on the floor, still in line. "Time to wake up!" Carefully, they get back on their knees, taking hold of feet, and slowly slide around the room. "OK, snake, come on home." The children all snake back into a circle and sit on the rug with legs crossed and knees touching. One child is slightly outside the circle, head down. Susie says: "Mrs. Smith, Fred isn't sticking together." Mrs. Smith: "Well, tell him." Susie: "Fred, you're not sticking with us. You've got to stick together." And Fred moves into the circle. But he seems sad, and his head is still down. Mrs. Smith: "Uh-oh, Fred looks like he has a problem. Are you OK? Did you get hurt when we played snake?" Fred shakes his head yes. Mrs. Smith: "Oh, no! What got hurt?" Fred shows us his hands, which may have gotten pinched by Lois' foot. Mrs. Smith, "Lois, you know what he needs, don't you?" Lois says, "He needs some lotion." And Lois takes some lotion and rubs it gently on Fred's hand and says, "Does it feel better?" Fred says: "Yes." Now he's smiling, head up and ready to participate. You feel relieved that he feels better.

You move on, back to a special education room. But these are big kids. You are visiting an intermediate learning disabilities room with children aged ten to thirteen. Maybe you'll see something you are more familiar with, more used to. You peek into the room. The class is on the floor with two teachers. Two children are in the middle of the circle, facing each other, sitting on the floor, holding hands with knees bent. They are looking straight at each other, waiting. One teacher says: "Are you ready?" The two in the middle say "Yup!" Then the whole group says: "Get ready—get set—GO!" And with this cue, the two in the middle smoothly pull up into a standing position, to the applause of all.

Now the questions are racing through your mind. Why so much play here? Give me the rationale! Give me the theory! Is this something special? Does it have a name? You want an explanation.

But there is one more class to see. Another special education room with about ten children aged six to eight, a teacher, an aide, and a group leader who has one child in her lap. One child is walking around the outside of the circle of children, tapping heads. You know this game. It's Duck-Duck-Goose. Right, but with one special modification. The head tapper says — "Goose!" — but instead of starting a chase, he runs one way and the Goose runs the other way until they meet and — HUG! — with big smiles on their faces. When this game is over, the group quiets down for the end of the session. The leader takes a pretzel from a bag and says: "Ready for a real funny one? This one's for you, Carl." And she tilts her head back and puts the pretzel on her chin. The class reacts, laughing: "Oh, no! Oh, no!" But Carl does not hesitate. He stands up, opens his mouth, and eats the pretzel right off the leader's chin! No hands! There are laughs around the room. What is this? The leader says: "Your turn, Carl." Now Carl has to think of a funny way to give a treat to his neighbor, Lisa. Copying the leader, he tries to put another pretzel on his own chin, but he cannot keep his head tilted for long enough and it keeps falling off! So he puts it on his elbow instead. Leader: "Oh, good idea!" Lisa laughs and bends over to eat the pretzel off Carl's elbow. So continues the pretzel eating around the circle until everyone has had a chance to eat one off a funny body part. Then everyone sings, "If you're happy and you know it, give a hug." And the group is over.

What is going on here? You have happened to arrive at these classrooms at Theraplay Group time. And of course, you have questions about all this. You hope someone is around to answer them. Well, that is why we are here. That is what this book is about. Now that you have had a taste of and peek at Theraplay Groups in classrooms, read on to find out what? why? and how?

Chapter 2

THE THERAPLAY® PRINCIPLE

Theraplay[1] was developed by Dr. Ann Jernberg, founder and clinical director of The Theraplay Institute, Chicago, Illinois (1979). It is a short-term therapeutic technique with roots in object relations theory, self-psychology, psychoanalysis and developmental psychology. The basic aim of Theraplay is to replicate the healthy parent/infant relationship. It is based in part on the work of Austin DesLauriers (1962, 1969) who stressed intrusiveness and physical contact in his efforts to establish relationships with schizophrenic and autistic children.

Theraplay is a structured, intensive, physical, individual therapy, using the type of play activities that characterize the healthy parent-infant relationship. There is little discussion. Instead, the focus is on pleasurable activities that will enable the child to **experience** the relationship with the adult. In Theraplay, the priority is on **personal interaction** (Jernberg, pg. 52), and thus, although there may be a few "props", there is minimal use of material objects (pg. 55). Rather, it is the therapist's and child's **selves** which are primarily used (pg. 54). As is characteristic of parent/infant play, fun and surprise (pg. 54) are used to keep the child engaged in the relationship. As is also true of parents and infants, it is the adult, not the baby, who is "in charge." (pg. 50–51)

Theraplay is in dynamic contrast to child-directed play therapy,[2] and should not be confused with it.

> In contrast to traditional play therapy, the Theraplay approach does not use props or toys or encourage the child to act out unconscious issues. The Theraplay therapist does not relate past experiences to the current interaction, or use inquiry in an attempt to elicit reflections or insights; he or she does not offer interpretations. In Theraplay there is no room for non-directive responses such as those associated with the Axline model of child therapy. Theraplay, instead, emphasizes the current relationship and offers a level of intimacy not evidenced in other prevailing forms of child psychotherapy. (Golden, 1983)

All infants have certain basic requirements for healthy development within the parent-child relationship. Theraplay conceptualizes these requirements under the terms Nurture, Intrusion/Stimulation, Structure, and Challenge, all taking place in as playful an atmosphere as possible.

A good parent:

1. **nurtures** her child: i.e., feeds, bathes, rocks, and comforts him
2. **intrudes** by stimulating her child to attend to the environment: i.e., plays peek-a-boo, gives piggy-back rides, plays "This little piggy"
3. **structures**: i.e., makes rules, says "No," keeps her child from danger
4. **challenges** her child to grow and learn: i.e., helps him to stand up, encourages his first step.

Theraplay sessions involve a focus on one or more of these areas, depending on the specific needs of each child. The therapist carefully evaluates each child in interaction with his family to develop a custom-tailored treatment plan. Activities are specifically chosen not only to provide intervention in one of the four major areas, but also to provide:

1. The element of "fun," spontaneity, and frivolity and
2. The focus on body contact, whether it be vigorous, playful, and competitive or tender, soothing, and nurturing. (Jernberg, pg. 21)

In a typical Theraplay session, the therapist may discover a child's muscle and demonstrate that the child is strong enough to push the therapist over; find a freckle right under a sparkling blue eye; turn around a resistive "no" with a song about "No, no, no!"; and put powder all over two little feet. A child who is withdrawing with hands over his face may become engaged by the therapist's discovery of a little pink ear on one side—and another one over there! Always the emphasis is on engaging the child, surprising him with something that is fun. Always the child will experience pleasurable activities with the therapist who knows well what a special person he is. Engaging the child in these interactions provides experiences that meet the child's needs in the four Theraplay areas, guiding him in learning to develop healthy relationships with others.

THE FIVE ELEMENTS OF THERAPLAY

Element #1: The Adult is in Charge

As a basic principle in recreating the parent-infant relationship in Theraplay, the adult is always in charge of the session.

We all know that for the safety, protection, and growth of the infant, the parent must be in charge. A six month old may resist having his snowsuit put on, or taking his medicine, but the good parent insists on it. Indeed, it is at least partly through experiencing the security of the adult's control that infants are able to establish trust and begin to develop autonomy. In like manner—in a very positive way—the Theraplay therapist gives the child the security of the therapist's control of the session.

During a Theraplay session, it is the therapist who makes the decisions about what is going to happen. The therapist decides what activities will be, what modifications will be made, and how the games will be played. Although this sounds "teacherish" and unpleasantly authoritarian, the Theraplay therapist does this with so much playfulness, all the while joining with the child in this play, that it feels as different from the teacher/student relationship as does the proverbial day and night! The therapist being in charge means that she might swoop the child up for a ride to the therapy room, pick him up on his legs to play airplane, or place him in her lap for a song. If she wants the child to run to her across the room, she will give the cue to run with directions such as, "Get ready, get set, GO!" The Theraplay therapist never asks the child, "Now what do you want to do?" or "Let's play patticake, OK?" Just like a parent, the therapist knows what is good for the child and does not ask his permission or opinion. She does not sit back and watch, but takes charge to actively involve the child in healthy interactions.

Traditional therapists may see a conflict among the issues of the therapist being in charge, being responsive to the child's needs, and the child's right to independence. We have all seen parents who have this same conflict. They let their children make all the decisions, down to what they eat and when they go to bed. What a burden this is to put on a small child! And we all know the result: The child eats junk food and goes to bed at midnight leaving behind miserable and frustrated parents who end up giving their child a message of anger and irritation, rather than of love and caring. These parents think that they will stifle the child if they decide things for him. But what happens is that the child takes over, and in so doing becomes highly anxious and insecure. The message that he gets from his parents is that they are not strong enough (or do not care enough about him) to protect him. These parents have confused the child's right to autonomy with independence from parental guidance. An adolescent can legitimately begin exploring independence. The one or two year old needs parental protection and guidance.[3] When the child is about to run out into the street, he does NOT need reasoning and independence, he needs to be STOPPED. He needs his parent to respond to his REAL need for protection, rather than his expressed wish for freedom.

We believe that when therapy is viewed as a replication of the parent/infant relationship as it is in Theraplay, there is no conflict between control and responsiveness—that indeed, one depends on the other.

It is the very fact that the Theraplay therapist is responsive to the underlying needs of the child, rather than to his overtly expressed wishes, that requires the therapist to take charge in order to create security. When the therapist senses a need in the child (fear, over-stimulation), the therapist does not wait for permission, nor does she ask the child what is wrong or if he needs help. The therapist ACTS. She responds in a way that will help the child. In fact, the child may resist, but the therapist responds **to the need** and persists in giving him healthy messages. For instance, a child may yawn and have trouble keeping his eyes open during a session, but protest that he is not tired. The therapist will insist that he is, rock him and soothe him to help him sleep. A child with scratches may act tough, saying the hurts do not hurt. The therapist checks them anyway, conveying the message that **any** hurt is important to care for. The therapist MUST duplicate for the child the experience of the infant being cared for by the healthy parent—i.e., the adult in charge of meeting the child's needs.

Element #2: Nurturing

The primary need of a new person-baby is to be nurtured: to have his basic needs met by a competent, caring person without his having to ask for it. A child who has experienced such caring will feel loved, important, responded to, safe, and comfortable, and will begin to respond to his caregiver-parent. He will establish eye contact with her, search for her when she leaves, reach for her, and eventually want to verbally communicate with her (Jernberg, 1979, pg. 5). He will transfer this safe and comfortable feeling to the rest of the world as his world expands. He will be able to trust new people (relatives, teachers, friends), and will eventually have the capacity to care for and empathize with others.

Nurturing is a significant element in Theraplay therapy with almost all children. The exceptions to this rule are those who have been overprotected and "babied" to the extent that their emotional growth has been retarded. (In such cases, other elements are emphasized.) Nurturing is expressed through deliberately caring activities, such as lotioning tummies, hands, feet, and noses and **feeling** and smelling that soft, wet stuff as the therapist rubs it in as though the child were a baby. Typically, a Theraplay therapist will end a session with a special song in honor of the child, with the child cradled in the therapist's lap like a baby, gazing up into the therapist's eyes. Or they might share a treat by feeding each other with their hands. In the event a bump or a scratch occurs during the session, or if the child comes in with a sore, the therapist immediately responds to it with concern and might gently rub lotion or powder around the "hurt," as we have come to call it. Whether small or large, a hurt does not go unnoticed or uncared for. The child must feel totally cared for throughout the entire session, no matter what the activity. Nurturing is the non-verbal, concrete expression of "I care about you."

Element #3: Stimulation

Jernberg calls this element of Theraplay "intrusion," but we feel that "stimulation" better describes what this message is about. Essentially, it is all about touching, surprising, activating, and exciting the child to respond to you. For the baby, these activities allow him to come in contact with a world other than himself, to explore it, and to differentiate himself from others in it. Stimulation "wakes him up" to the world outside himself, encourages curiosity, and gets him moving toward others. When Mommy nibbles his feet, hides and surprises during peek-a-boo, when Daddy skillfully throws him in the air and catches him, the baby feels excitement, pleasure sometimes mixed with anticipation of the unknown, and delight that the world is still safe, as well as exciting and inviting. His self-esteem and confidence increase when he feels the pleasure the adults are getting from playing with him. Through these activities with his loving parents, the child is shown that it is OK to venture out, to explore the world, to grow, and to try new things.

Like a parent, the Theraplay therapist also plays peek-a-boo and patticake, gives leg rides and slides, tickles, rubs noses, swings the child, and may "throw" the child into his parent's arms. These playful activities that involve body contact, disappearing and appearing into the child's view, and pleasant sensory surprises recreate those early activities necessary for development of healthy self concept. They help the child to differentiate himself from the therapist, to see the world as inviting, and himself as appealing. In the words of Phyllis Booth of The Theraplay Institute, the child "must come to see, reflected in the therapist's eyes, the image of himself both as lovable and as fun to be with." (Jernberg, 1979, pg. 3).

Element #4: Structure

For a child, life is not all "fun and games." Structure is also present. While the mother is being playful and nurturing, she is at the same time giving messages about rules. One could say that the first structuring message the mother gives to her baby is that she (the adult) is in charge. This differentiates adult from child and allows the child to BE a child, rather than a small grown-up. Thus the child will be able to understand his role with others in his future such as his teachers, relatives, babysitters, etc.

Parental structure keeps the baby safe. There are limits and boundaries within which the child must stay. If he should venture beyond them, Mom and Dad quickly come to bring him back to safety. The baby crawling toward the stairs is picked up and carried some distance from the stairs. If he reaches for the electric socket, Mom yells, "No!" and moves him away. At this young age, structure is conveyed primarily through physical movement and guidance: non-verbal structuring. But parents also structure their baby as they play with him. We do not recognize this as structure, probably because it is done in such a playful manner. But, in fact, when Mom is nibbling her baby's feet, and her baby starts to put his feet in his own mouth, and Mom says playfully, "Give me those feet!" and opens her mouth in readiness, she is bringing her baby back into the structure of her game with him. When the baby gives Mom his feet, he is responding and complying with her structure because he knows it is going to be pleasurable and fun. He also knows that complying with Mom does not mean a loss of self-esteem because he has experienced that play with his Mom actually **enhances** his self-esteem.

As the child grows, structure is more frequently conveyed in ways we more easily recognize: i.e., through limits, rules, restrictions, and social conventions. We forget that it can be conveyed through play and we begin to think of structure as serious and un-fun. However, for children who have difficulty with issues of structuring, the Theraplay therapist, like the parent, incorporates structure into the fun and games of the session. There are limits and boundaries to the session, the therapy area, and the games. Welcoming and closing activities define a clear start and finish to the sessions. There is a Theraplay area (a mat, room, etc.), and there are general "rules" to each activity. But the unique quality of Theraplay becomes evident when the child ventures beyond these boundaries. How is structure conveyed in a non-punitive, accepting, esteem-enhancing manner? Here is how:

The therapist and child are playing. The child turns and begins to run out the door. The therapist goes after him, swoops him up and says playfully, "Come back here! I want to play with you! Now here we go! Up on my knees for a ride!" quickly structuring him into a new and interesting game. Now, of course, we all know some children who will decide that what is actually fun and daring is to defy the therapist and attempt to run out the door again. Such a child, after a few captures, will, with a twinkle in his eye, go for the door again. This is the child who needs help with structuring. The therapist then conveys firmness: "Hey, you keep running away. We have to stay in here. Here is where we play. Now I am going to help you stay with me so we can play some more." And with that, the therapist holds the child's hand, or plops him in her lap, and with the non-verbal structure of physical touch, involves the child in another, pleasurable game.

Another time, the therapist wants the child to run to her across the room. This is a particularly structuring activity in that there is a specific action the child is told to do and a special time for him to do it. The therapist directs the child to stand at one end of the room: "OK, now I'm going over there and I want you to run right into my arms. I'm going to catch you! Now, wait until I tell you to run. Get ready, get set, RUN!" and the child dashes across the room into the arms of the therapist who swoops him up into a triumphant hug. The child has stayed within the structure of the game. But what if the child does not do this? What if, as the therapist is saying, "Get ready," the child impulsively or purposefully starts to run, ignoring the therapist's cue? "Hey!" the therapist may say, "You didn't wait for me to say, 'RUN!'" and the therapist catches the child, giving him a playful tickle as she puts him back into position and restructures. "You have to wait until I say, 'RUN.' I'm going to say, 'Get ready, get set, RUN.' Can you do it? Of course you can! OK. Here we go!" And they happily try it again. Often the Theraplay therapist uses paradoxical or challenging techniques to bring the child into the therapist's structure so that the child can continue to benefit from the positive and esteem-building interactions. These are discussed further in Chapter 13.

Certainly, one of the unique characteristics of a Theraplay therapist, in addition to a readiness to be nurturing and playful, is the ability to persist in restructuring and bringing the child constantly back into the interaction. Theraplay provides a wide variety of techniques that the therapist can use with the withdrawn and isolated child as well as with the mischievously difficult child described above.

Element #5: Challenge

"Why did the man climb the mountain? Because it was there." So goes the old joke. And we do it all the time. We learn to skate and ski. We learn to drive. We visit new places, try new foods, meet new people, get new jobs. Why? Not just because they are there, but because they challenge us. Facing challenges can be exciting. Being successful at a challenging task can bring fulfillment and a great sense of competence. For these reasons, challenge is an essential part of life.

We can see this when we watch even the small child. He struggles. He falls. He bumps his nose and knees. Yet he keeps persisting until he walks. He builds, and stacks, and assembles until finally his tower stands. Out on the playground, he watches the others go up the slide, walks up to it, walks away, walks up again, and his mother says, "Let's go up. Come on." She encourages, helps, protects, while urging him to climb up and then slide down into her waiting arms. And then he cannot be stopped! How exciting life is when you feel you have mastered an unknown, new experience! You feel just plain good.

Challenge is an important aspect of Theraplay sessions, but especially with children who are particularly fearful of new experiences. Taking the child's hands in hers, the therapist might playfully say, "Bet you can't push me down on the mat. Now I'm going to rub those muscles for good luck. OK. Get ready, get set, (always structuring at the same time), GO! Wow! You did it." Even with the littlest push, the therapist has fallen down, gets up with eyes wide in admiration of the child's impressive strength, and encourages him to do it again, but **harder.** Or she might use paradox to playfully encourage the child to come out of his shell. For a child who hardly moves unless told to, she might begin to move away from the child and say, "Don't come get me. Stay right there. Don't catch me." And the therapist does whatever she has to do, non-verbally, to get the child to move slightly toward her and touch, and the game has begun. This frightened, stiff child begins to go after the therapist with a big, triumphant smile. How great it feels to be encouraged to come out of that shell! The child was just waiting for someone to help him do it.

However, some people say, "We must wait for the child to be ready for our interactions." "One should not just go up to a child and start playing with him." "Give him time to get to know you first," they say. Psychological theory, child development theory, and the Theraplay philosophy stress the importance of the passage of time in the child's life. The longer the healthy messages are missing, the longer it takes to "make up" the loss. In fact, researchers are now suggesting that some losses can never be made up. The **child** cannot afford to wait until we think he is ready for us to give him what he needs. Once again, we must **take charge.**

Thus, it is by establishing healthy interactions with the therapist during shared play such as we have described, that Theraplay meets the child's underlying needs and promotes healthier functioning. Because these interactions are pleasurable, the child learns to, and wants to, engage in other relationships in a positive way.

While we feel that the rationale for Theraplay establishes its role as a therapeutic technique, it does not negate the need for, and appropriateness of, other child therapies. Jernberg specifies that Theraplay is not appropriate for the traumatized child, the "fragile" child, the sociopathic child, or the abused child (Jernberg, 1979, pg. 26–32). Also, other therapies may be appropriate at various times during one child's treatment. We appreciate the importance of flexibility in therapy. No **one** therapy can be a panacea.

ENDNOTES

1. Theraplay has been registered as a Service Mark. One must have received the required training in order to call the therapy that he does, "Theraplay."
2. Non-directive play therapy is a client-centered approach to working with children. Play materials such as a doll house, cars, dolls, toy animals, playhouse materials, telephones, clay, and paints, are provided to allow the children to enact and express difficult issues.

The therapist only sets limits when there is the possibility of physical harm, but otherwise does not direct the children's play.

3. We recognize that two year olds are developing autonomy and that they need to begin making their own choices. However, this must be done under the loving guidance of parents since young children still need external structure.

Chapter 3

THE EVOLUTION OF THERAPLAY GROUPS

EARLY GROUPS

Viola Brody (1976) developed an approach to working with groups of children based on principles very similar to those of Theraplay. Her approach, called Developmental Play, "was established on the rationale that personal development, cognitive functioning and expressive communication in young children can be enhanced through play experiences with persons who become important to the children." (Brody, pg. 5)

> Although the focus is on play and not school work, it is a structured program in which participants (first child to adult and then child to child) get to know each other by having a good time together. In addition to having fun, the children are encouraged to become aware of and to express their feelings. When successfully implemented the Developmental Play program creates an atmosphere of a large family whose members experience warmth, caring and openness with each other. (Brody, pg. 5).

Brody conducted her Developmental Play program with children in kindergarten, first, and second grades. Each group included from six to eight children with an equal number of adults so that each child would be able to develop a special relationship with his own adult. The sessions began with a period of one-to-one child to adult play. Next came a group activity time (Circle Time), and the session ended with a snack. The relationship between adult and child was the primary focus, and the couple stayed together whether or not they chose to participate in the group activity.

Jernberg's (1979, Chapter 4) groups were much different from Brody's, although the activities were similar, if not the same. She used two trained Theraplay therapists with from four to eight children approximately the same ages (pg. 130). Two co-therapists allowed the group to replicate a two-parent family, and also allowed (as in traditional therapeutic situations) one therapist to talk **to** and the other therapist to talk **for** the child. Her groups were designed for children who had difficulty relating to peers: those who could not share with others, who hesitated making relationships with others, and who were uncomfortable with intimacy (pg. 126). Developed in a private therapy setting in which the therapists had control over which clients would be part of which group, Jernberg recommended that, "Each participant should [have] in common with at least one other child his particular problem in relating (for example, pseudoconfidence, quarrelsomeness, excessive shyness, or over-competitiveness)." (pg. 130) Theraplay groups were controlled by the therapists who decided the activities for each session and handled problem behavior. Activities were within each child's abilities, and each session focused on one problem. Jernberg's groups began with an introduction and greetings, continued with a period of active games that tapered into quiet and more intimate activities, and ended with a song or snack (pg. 131–132). All games were intrusive, intense, and surprising. The children were never allowed to leave the scene, nor were they kept out of activities because of poor interactive skills. Instead the therapist would stop the activity to help a child respond appropriately to the activity. As the children became more able to relate to each other, role playing was also done.

BEGINNINGS OF CLASSROOM GROUPS

In 1981, in the Proviso Area for Exceptional Children (PAEC) special education cooperative, we began applying and adapting Theraplay principles to a group situation in special education classrooms. The idea of doing so arose when children receiving individual Theraplay needed a group experience; at the same time there were classrooms in which several children needed a Theraplay experience but not necessarily individual Theraplay. It was therefore decided to see if classroom Theraplay Groups could indeed be used to meet these complementary needs.

The PAEC Theraplay Group program incorporated aspects of both Brody's and Jernberg's approaches along with new ideas that arose from our special setting. We neither had one adult for each child, nor could we choose who was to be in our groups. We did not have a therapy room, but rather held the groups in the special education classroom itself, necessitating the cooperation and involvement of the teacher.

Running a group in another teacher's room posed problems that resulted in significant changes in the Theraplay Group process. It became clear that the intrusive, stimulating games which were quite effective in individual Theraplay had their drawbacks in the school setting where more control is expected, and where children may need more structure around transitions. Thus, we began to refine the activities to reflect the need for a high level of structure. Rules were developed to help set the structure and atmosphere of the groups: NO HURTS; STICK TOGETHER; and HAVE FUN. (We will explain these rules in Chapter 5.) We structured the activities: 99% of the games were done in a circle and, in general, the children were not allowed to move away from the group and around the room. This sometimes required an adaptation of a game that was generally less structured. We also began sharing the leadership of the groups with social workers and teachers.

The social workers added a qualitative dimension to the potential of our Theraplay Groups. Although a characteristic Theraplay session is bigger on action than on talk, we found that the children were able and willing to raise heretofore difficult topics and to share feelings, support, and suggestions as they felt increasingly safe, accepted, and trusted by the group. It was through social worker Diane Mirabito, who had a natural instinct to seize any opportunity for such discussions, that we realized that the atmosphere we created could meet the needs of a variety of special educators, and not just the Theraplay therapist.

As a result of this collaboration of professionals, Theraplay Groups were successfully implemented in classes for the learning disabled, the behavior disordered, and cross-categorical classes which included mentally handicapped and language disordered children. The ages of the children in these groups ranged from three to thirteen years.

The teachers who tried these groups in their rooms felt that the children benefited from being together in a relaxed environment while still having to get along with each other. At times, the teachers were surprised by behaviors that they had never seen occur in the regular academically-oriented classroom setting. We realized that, in this rather intimate, family-like group, the children were reacting more as they might with their own family or in other purely social situations. Problem behaviors surfaced that had not been seen in the classroom before but that parents or other school staff had been concerned about. The Theraplay Group provided a structured social setting in which these behaviors could manifest themselves and be dealt with constructively by supportive adults and peers. It became clear that this technique was meeting a real need in the classroom.

TRAINING FOR LEADING THERAPLAY GROUPS WITH CHILDREN

As time went on, your authors teamed up to present talks on Theraplay Groups to special education professionals, school social workers, speech and language therapists, and early childhood specialists. Our audience responded enthusiastically to the possibility of using this new technique with their children. At PAEC, we continued to hear from teachers that they found great value in our classroom Theraplay Groups. Three non-Theraplay-therapists, after informal training, were now leading their own groups. We became convinced that a training program, less intensive than that required to be a Theraplay therapist, could train professionals to lead Theraplay Groups. With the support of The Theraplay Institute, we began to develop a formal training program for professionals with no prior Theraplay background. After completing this program, these professionals **would not be Theraplay therapists,** but would be qualified to lead Theraplay Groups with children.

In February, 1986, the first eight trainees began the process of training. This involved an introductory workshop, an intermediate workshop (approximately two days each), and a ten month supervision period. During this ten month period, the trainees led their own groups, videotaped at least one session per month, and participated in a supervision session of two hours per month which involved a review of the tape.

The make-up of this first group of 8 people was most interesting. Five were special education teachers. Their classes covered non-categorical preschool, developmental kindergarten, primary and intermediate severely learning disabled, and autistic children. One of these teachers was already leading her own group since she had co-led a group with Rubin for two years. However, she had no formal background in the Theraplay philosophy. The sixth person was the aide to one of the preschool teachers. Her interest and involvement taught us that including the aide in the workshops with the teacher she was working with, could help them learn how to work together leading their Group.

We were surprised and delighted when two regular education teachers signed up. One taught kindergarten, the other first grade. We wondered to ourselves whether this type of group would really be possible in the regular classroom with many more children and no aide. But the two teachers insisted that they were willing to try, because their children seemed to need something that they otherwise could not give or even understand. These two teachers seemed to soak up the information, and they could not wait to start their groups. The reports they brought back of their children's responses and the carry-over that occurred after only two group sessions, amazed even those of us who knew that Theraplay Groups had a lot to offer. One of these teachers, Mary Alice DaCosse, has shared her experiences and her philosophy about the need for such groups in regular education. These are included in Chapter 11.

Another one of the eight teachers, Susan Noble Pelafas, completed the entire training process (workshops and supervision) with her class of autistic children, and was the first certified leader of Theraplay Groups with children to come out of this training program. We had originally thought that Sue's class could not handle a group, but we did not discourage her from trying. We were amazed at the response of autistic children to a Theraplay Group. During the year and a half of the training program, Sue observed exciting changes in her class. Some of these experiences are shared in Appendix 1.

Each of the people involved in our training program remained enthusiastic about the use of Theraplay Groups with their classes. Our belief that teachers could successfully learn to lead their own groups by participating in workshops and supervision was confirmed. Thus a new phase of Theraplay in the classroom was born and validated.

In this book, we want to share with you the knowledge we have gained from our experience both in leading Theraplay Groups in classrooms, and in training others to lead these groups.

Chapter 4

WHY USE THERAPLAY GROUPS
IN YOUR CLASSROOM?

These groups look really different. They look different not only because of the play and informality involved, but also because problems continually arise during the sessions. You not only have the struggles and frustrations that come with trying a new technique, but the technique itself will keep you confronted with problem behaviors!

We can hear you saying, "I've got enough to do already. This better be good for me to try it!"

We think it is! And so do other professionals who have used Theraplay Groups with their children. Each of them has a different way of describing what is special and valuable about Theraplay Groups in the classroom, and we will try to summarize their ideas here.

First of all, if the children, or even **one** child, in your class should need emotional support and help, this is a way for help to reach more at one time. A group can never be a substitute for individual therapy if that is what a child really needs. But a Theraplay Group **is** a way for many adjustment, social, and security needs to be addressed in the class with all involved. For children who feel frightened, timid, unloved, who need a bit more attention than their family can give them, who may express this by being aggressive or withdrawn—Theraplay Groups give them the opportunity to express these feelings, rather than continue to hold them in. Providing a group that allows these feelings to come out tells the children it is OK to let them out. Letting them out in a healthy, supportive environment, with an understanding, guiding adult present, can go a long way toward building mental health and contributing to better school adjustment and academic functioning.

We are not talking about **just** letting the feelings out but about dealing with the **underlying issues** that are expressed in both feelings and behaviors. Indeed, the main point of a Theraplay Group is exactly this: to allow problems to surface in a nurturing atmosphere, rather than being suppressed and controlled, only to pop out at another time.

A Theraplay Group makes a family out of your class. It can develop greater understanding between the children, more awareness of each child as a unique and special individual with both strengths and weaknesses, and can increase the children's tolerance of differences. In becoming a **healthy** family, the children will learn to get along with others, to stand up for themselves as well as others, to care about each other, to be honest about their feelings, and to support others with constructive criticism, empathy, and nurturing.

A Theraplay Group is a very different approach to working on social skills. It does not resemble the "structured teaching" classroom in any way and that is one of its major advantages. It provides relief for everybody from the typical school routine, and because it is playful, the children are open and responsive to it. But within this inviting, welcoming playfulness, the children are still "learning" something! They are giving and receiving empathy, they are becoming aware of how they get along with others and can try new ways. Using a totally different and non-teaching approach goes a long way to promote carry-over for any new skill learned. This is more like real life and the feelings and interactions here can more easily be integrated into the child's life.

So what does this have to do with teaching or education? Your job is to **teach,** not to worry about the children's social life, isn't it?

Ask yourself these questions: How much time do you spend handling **"discipline"**? How much energy does it take you to "motivate" your students or to "control" your class? How many times has your reading class been interrupted by a scuffle in the back of the room or the outbreak of a squabble—"Teacher! He broke my pencil!"

The fact is that children are **not** compartmentalized. Their problems, feelings and needs are always affecting their behavior and their learning. When we become more aware of, and attend to, their emotional needs, we will find that the children begin both to control their own behavior and to learn more academically.

Isn't this really what we want for our children?

Chapter 5

CREATING THE THERAPLAY ATMOSPHERE

Let us warn you that creating the Theraplay atmosphere is probably the most difficult aspect of this technique both to **do** and to explain! You must leave behind what you have been trained to do as a teacher, speech and language therapist, and parts of what you have been trained to do even if you are a social worker or counselor. You will gain new ways of looking at your children, new ways to recognize their needs, and new ways of responding to them. This technique can only enhance your effectiveness in the classroom by giving you more alternatives for dealing with problems.

We will describe the task of creating the Theraplay Group and show how the four rules for the group help foster a healthy atmosphere.

UNLEARNING; OR: HOW TO STOP TEACHING

The first requirement for the Theraplay Group leader is to stop teaching. Only then will you be able to pass along the healthy Theraplay messages in your group. The important messages each child must receive while he is in the group are that he is accepted, wanted, important, and cared-for. The first two may be the hardest to learn to do, since often we are upset, disappointed, and frustrated with individual children. These are especially difficult issues if you are a classroom teacher who is at the same time the leader of the group. You have spent the whole day with your class and may not feel so accepting of a particular child because of events that have happened during the day.

These issues are not just hard for the teacher, however. Educators have been taught to exclude children from pleasant activities if their behavior is not up to standards. When a child who we know can do better has had a bad day, does poor work, or shows poor social judgment, we become frustrated with him, our self image as a competent teacher is shattered, and we verbally or non-verbally show him that we are disappointed and dissatisfied with him because he has not performed up to par. When a child is agitated, preoccupied, or visibly frightened, we try to tell him he should be a "big boy," to "not worry" or "not be scared," and we remind him to get his mind back on the task at hand.

So well trained are we not to deal with inner emotional issues, that we do not even stop to find out that perhaps he witnessed his parents fighting and is confused and worried about divorce. Perhaps his mother yelled at him as he left for school that morning. Possibly there is violence or the threat of it in his family. Perhaps there is little nurturing in the home and the mother has sent her four year old to school with no lunch or even breakfast. The "immature" behaviors that we try to modify may be caused by real turmoil and confusion in the child's life. Having a child in special education, which virtually labels him as "abnormal," creates a strain on the family which results in conflicts that in turn further affect the child's well-being. There are times when we should look to the emotional issues involved and then respond to the real anxiety that is causing him to behave the way he does.

The Theraplay Group provides the format for uncovering these issues by conveying the same messages a parent would convey to her young child. These are:

1. I accept you even if you are having trouble right now, and I **will show you** by sticking with you and helping you cope. I will not abandon you.
2. I want to be with you and I want you to be with me, and I **will show you** by bringing you into my activities and by joining you in yours.
3. You are important in my eyes, and I **will show you** by appreciating anything you make, say, or do, and by listening to you and believing in what you say.
4. I will take care of you when you need caring. Even if you do not let on that you need caring, I will know and be there for you.

Just as the mother cannot just **say** these things to her young child, but must **show** him by her actions, so are these messages demonstrated by our actions in the group. This is how the feeling of "family" is recreated in a Theraplay Group.

RULES OF THE THERAPLAY GROUP

To help us give these messages to the children and set the stage for them to give these messages to each other, we have developed three rules for Theraplay Groups: NO HURTS—STICK TOGETHER—HAVE FUN. And there is one implicit Theraplay rule that will be familiar to you from the elements of Theraplay: THE ADULT IS IN CHARGE.

The Adult is in Charge

Remember what the parent being in charge does for the child?

This makes his world safe, gives him a sense of security, gives him the message that he is important. He learns his parent cares about him so much that she will do with her child, or for her child, what he needs, **regardless of whether or not he has asked for it.**

So, the Theraplay Group leader is also in charge. Often, this is not an announced rule. But it is clear from the start by the manner in which the therapist leads the group. She never asks the group what they want to do, or when they want to do it, or if the game she planned is OK. She simply gets the class involved and begins. "OK. Everybody get ready because we're going to do something very special today. We're going to hold hands and sit on the rug in a circle. Let's go! I'll take Ronny's hand, Ronny you take Susie's hand, Susie get Kathy, etc." And she guides them toward the rug to sit together cozily. Even in the way she starts each new activity, there is no question that this is an adult-directed group. "OK, did everybody bring their muscles? I hope so, because you're going to need them. Let's check to see. Hold them up there. Good. Hey, Bobby, you didn't bring any today? We have to find you some, because you need them for this game, and we can't play without you. Let's all give Bobby a little of our muscles so he can play." And she starts by rubbing her muscles on Bobby's upper arms, then giving all the children a chance to do the same. "Wow! I'm so glad we found you some muscles. Now, get ready to use them." And the leader proceeds to involve the class in a game of Partner Pull-ups.

The children feel **secure** that the leader can **and will** handle problems when they come up. They feel **important** because she has brought a game for all of them to play and that she will play **with** them. They feel **relieved** when she finds a way to involve Bobby, because it **shows** (not tells) them that when **they** need her, she will recognize it and help them too.

This sense of security and trust in the therapist will extend toward other members in the group and provide the foundation for the children to begin to reach out to each other.

No Hurts

No Hurts is the rule that:

1. allows us to nurture the children whether or not they ask for it; and
2. helps us make sure no one ever gets hurt—no matter how mildly— during the group experience.

At its most obvious level, when children come in with scratches, illness, hunger, etc., we immediately respond to the "hurts" even (and especially) if they shrug them off as inconsequential. We must be sure that each child is getting the message somewhere (if not at home, then he must get it in this group) that an adult will see his pain or anxiety and take care of him without expecting him to be "a big boy" and swallow his discomfort. If "swallowing discomfort" occurs too often or at too young an age, the resulting behavior may be like that of Jimmy, who was hit in the head with a rock at school and did not respond or change expression or go for help even though his head was bleeding. He had learned that no one would respond to his needs, so he deadened himself to the pain. Children like Jimmy are in real danger of neglecting themselves or allowing others to abuse them.

When we notice children's hurts, we model what they should be feeling by our words, actions, and expression. "Oh, another hurt? Boy, that's a big scratch! It must have hurt real bad. What happened?" And we bring out the lotion or powder, showing the children how we carefully put it **around** the hurt. We explain why it must not go on top: because it is not medicine and it might sting and possibly even infect the wound.

There are many times when the hurt will not be so obvious, however. It may be an emotional rather than a physical hurt. The child may show such a hurt by being very wiggly. Or he may be disruptive, or unusually quiet. We notice these signals, and comment that Jimmy is having a hard time today in the group, and "Let's find out why." If asking Jimmy does not work, you can try asking the group, "Does anyone know why Jimmy doesn't feel good today?" As the children give ideas, keep checking with Jimmy to see if one of his friends has figured out what is bothering him.

Sometimes one will know, sometimes not. What follows is an example of what can happen:

Lou was giggly and laughing in an exaggerated manner at every interaction during one Theraplay session. After noticing this atypical behavior for quite a while, the leader commented that Lou was having trouble today, and asked, "What's going on?" Lou said that he did not know. Then the leader asked the group if anyone thought he might know what was troubling Lou. Some children had ideas, but Lou said, "No," that they had not understood what was troubling him. But, after all the guesses were over, Lou himself said that he was expecting a visit from his father who was divorced from his mother. He apparently had recurring ambivalent feelings about his father's visits, and his anticipation of this event signaled that he was struggling with some very difficult issues.

Now, in situations such as this, when it is obvious to others that something must be troubling a child, it is very likely that, when asked what the problem is, the child will not be able to express the true cause. Even in Lou's case, the true cause may not have been a visit from his father. Or, if a reason is given, it may not be the sole cause, since causes are often quite complicated. Therefore, it may be even wiser and more helpful to the child if, when you see signs of distress, you simply acknowledge that "Lou" is troubled today, and that we all might need to be more understanding of him today. Leave open the possibility of his talking about it. You might find that later on in the day, he brings up the true problem with you or another person. Be on the look-out for this.

Even though we have a No Hurts rule, there will be hurts that happen right in the group. During a game, a child (or adult) might get hurt, either accidentally or on purpose. The response of the adults and the group should be the same no matter why the hurt occurred. The game stops, the child is checked out (preferably by the person who hurt him, yet without making that person feel unduly guilty or frightened), and lotion may be applied (again preferably by the hurter). There will always be children who do not mention that they were hurt, but if you saw it happen, you must respond to it in the same way we wish Jimmy's mother would have done. Even if it was a trivial hurt, there should still be some response to it. If the child is all right, the game can continue with the challenge that we must do it with no hurts this time.

LEADER: Oops! Harry, Trish bumped you. Are you OK?

HARRY: It's OK. It didn't hurt.

LEADER: Wait, we have to check you anyway. Where did you get bumped? Here, on your shoulder? Let's take a look. It does look OK. Here's some lotion to make sure it will feel good. Trish, Harry will show you just where to put the lotion. Make sure it feels OK.

(After the lotioning:) OK. Now let's try that game again, but this time, no hurts. Trish, watch out for Harry, Harry watch out for Terry, Terry watch out for me, etc. Let's see if we can do it, 'cause hurts are no fun.

There might be some children in your group who make up hurts, or others who announce that they have hurts and keep finding more of them throughout the session. If a hurt is made up, you might tell the child that you cannot see it, but you will put some lotion on it anyway. Maybe the child remembers a past hurt, or it could mean that this particular child feels very vulnerable and can be easily hurt emotionally. **You** do not know why he needs the nurturing, but he has told you that he does. It would not help him to tell him his arm looks fine, and that he does not need any lotion. Can it really hurt him to be nurtured for a hurt that **you** cannot see? Of course not.

However, you may get a child who truly does have hurts, but so many of them that you could spend the whole session just with him! And what's more, he wants you to! Dealing with his problem is more complicated. He certainly needs nurturing. However, it is a tricky business with such children because they are often very manipulative, and tend to only want the nurturing on their own terms, both as a way to control the group and to get all the attention for themselves. How do you both provide the much needed nurturing, but keep the control in your hands? Some suggestions:

1. Express real concern over so many hurts. In our experience, it is useful to ask how he got so many hurts. He is either provoking hurts, purposely getting into situations in which he will get hurt, or being victimized or neglected by someone. Any of these behaviors indicates that he has low self-esteem and cannot imagine that things could be any different. It can be important to know what is going on.

2. Try challenging him to bring less hurts with him next time. For example:

LEADER: Ralph, my goodness, you have, let's see, seven hurts on this arm, five on the other arm, one on your nose, one on each knee, and two on your hand. That's, um, seventeen hurts! That's too many! Wonder if you can bring less hurts with you next week. Let's everybody remember, today Ralph had seventeen hurts. We'll count them next week. You've got to bring less next time. Think you can do it? We'll see! I hope so, 'cause seventeen hurts is too much for one kid.

3. Always attend to (i.e., lotion, blows, etc.) at least the biggest hurt. You can nurture lots of them quickly by blowing an arm, fanning a leg with a pillow, fanning the whole child at one time! You can also take a survey of the intact parts of the child: "Does your nose still wiggle? Does it hurt when I wiggle it? Do your fingers still work even with the hurt on your elbow? Thank goodness!"
4. Use this as a time to encourage asserting.

An example of this occurred in Tregay's class. Mannie was a very manipulative and demanding child. He alternated between looking for another of his many hurts throughout the session, and belittling a hurt that would actually happen during the session. He prided himself in saying things did not hurt; in fact, he said that he liked to get hurt. During one session, when Tregay asked where the hurts came from, Mannie said that his sister would threaten him and scratch him. Tregay said, "Tell your sister I said, 'No hurts!'" Months later, during another session, Mannie said, "Mrs. Tregay, my sister's trying to hurt me again. What was that you told me to tell her?" Slowly, but hopefully surely, this type of nurturing/asserting will build up the child's self-esteem so that he might be able to do his own asserting.

For children who seem to be deliberately hurting others, you can use the power of the group to challenge them to play the game by the NO HURTS rule:

LEADER: Wait a minute! Stan got hurt this time. Bet you can't do it again without one of you getting hurt.

BOYS DOING THE GAME: Yes we can. (Smiling mischievously.)

LEADER: I don't think so. What do you think, Paul? (And the leader goes around the group asking for "bets" on whether the two boys can cooperate constructively.)

Another example that evokes the No Hurts rule is when you see a child get hurt but he does not say anything. That is the time to:

1. Respond for the child because he cannot yet do it for himself:

   LEADER: OW! (With real concern on her face, as though she felt what the child **should have** felt.) That hurt! Let's look at it. Wow, that hurts! (stroking around it and watching to see if it gets red.)

2. Begin to help him express his needs by encouraging him to tell the hurter he was hurt.

   LEADER: Betty, Karl hurt you. Don't let him hurt you. You better tell him what happened.

   BETTY: (to Karl) You hurt me.

   LEADER: Better tell him not to hurt you next time.

   BETTY: Don't hurt me again. I don't like hurts.

Stick Together

Stick Together is the rule that keeps the children involved with each other, and demonstrates that we care about each other. We are saying to them: "I want you to be with me, and I want to be with you." Very simply, to carry this out, we include everyone in everything.

The group does not start until everyone in the room is in the circle, including the adults. This clearly shows you think that everyone is important and that the group would not be the same without each one of them—which is really true! If you repeatedly start without members of the group, you are telling the others that you would not delay the group for them either. This message will create insecurity—directly opposite to the Theraplay atmosphere you want. But we know that there are pressures that could cause you to start your group without members:

1. If a child is really stalling, am I letting him control the group by waiting for him?
2. If I delay the group for a staller/disrupter, won't other children try to do the same thing?
3. If I focus on the staller, won't others stall just to get my attention?
4. If the child is shy/frightened, shouldn't I start the group and let

him decide that he wants to join the fun? If I insist he join, won't that just make him more frightened?

Those are real questions, but questions that can too frequently cause you to leave a child out of the group. We do this all too often, rather than acting on our knowledge that his being in the group is the healthiest thing for him, and using every technique at our disposal to involve him. Thus, the first Theraplay rule is that everyone must **always** be included. In the long run, it will be detrimental to your group and to the child if you exclude him.

The questions raised above deal with children who might have a number of reasons for refusing to participate. Some children are simply being manipulative and controlling, some need to keep emotionally distant from others, some are fearful and withdrawn, and others shrink from physical contact. But each and every one of them needs and will benefit from your group. The techniques you use to involve them may differ, but you must always remember that, in showing you their issues, they are also showing you what they need from the group.

Let us look at each child more closely to understand what he needs and discuss some possible techniques for involving him.

The Non-Participator: Why, and What to Do

The manipulative child: The child who is manipulative will try to get us to "stand on our heads" to please him. So he becomes difficult and dissatisfied with everything. He wants to stop the group, and have all the attention focused on him. He probably runs the show at home as well, with everyone catering to him in hopes of keeping some peace in the house. He probably sees himself as difficult and a troublemaker, one who always causes problems. Older children, especially, may manipulate by refusing to join the group as a way to control and to dominate attention.

If you let the manipulative child destroy your group, you are repeating what is probably for him a typical experience. If you give in by excluding him from the group, he has gotten his way **and** the exclusion means that he is "bad"—after all, you do not want him. He needs firm structure, acceptance, nurturing, and for the adult to be in charge.

How can you involve him? You can challenge him. Older children especially need and want challenge. They want to "win" over us. You can "bet" him or the group that he will not join in. You can challenge him to help think of a way to make a game more fun, or harder.

If it is very obvious that he is being manipulative, you can very gently (nurturing) but firmly (structuring) insist that he has to join the group. If he is younger, you can physically bring him to the group. But you can also demonstrate acceptance at the same time, saying that he does not want to join the group (for whatever expressed reason) but that you want him to be with the group anyway. "That's too bad" if he does not want to join in, but he must **stay with** the group.

The distant child: The distant child shows little emotion and appears not to care about people or the group. In fact, he acts disinterested and distant to protect himself from getting too close and involved. He senses that if he got involved, he might be touched emotionally, and, being afraid of that, he keeps his distance both in mind and body. He has probably been hurt before in his relationships with important people in his life. Maybe there was a divorce or maybe there are family problems right now. Maybe when he was an infant or very young child, his parents were distant and uninvolved with him and thus he has never experienced an emotional tie with people. He has never felt closeness. Thus, closeness probably frightens him, and he has developed an air of indifference and coldness that keeps him emotionally apart from people, and causes people to want to keep their distance from him.

Distant children will remain distant unless someone who knows what they need attempts to bridge the distance, regardless of what the child seems to want. You can provide bridges by always including him in your group. His very presence and involvement in the relationship-building experiences of Theraplay may bring him closer to being touched emotionally—closer to being a whole and healthier person. So you must persist in your attempts to bring him into your group.

The withdrawn child: The withdrawn child will look as though he wishes he were invisible. He wishes we would forget about him and leave him alone. He looks so afraid that **we** become afraid to involve him! Shouldn't we wait until he is ready? If he is so afraid, won't we scare him if we go after him?

Can you remember a time or place when you were scared and timid, unable to bring yourself to get involved: in a dance? at a party? to speak up at a meeting? Remember how it felt to want to participate, but to almost feel stuck in your place, too afraid to make the first move? **But you wanted to!** Did it ever happen that someone came along to "give you the push"? Maybe a friend grabbed your hand and said, "Come on, dance with us!" Or at a party, the host said, "Come over here, I'd like you to meet _____, you both have something in common." And that was just what you needed to join in and feel a part of the group.

That is what the withdrawn and frightened child needs. Allowing him to remain alone sets the glue more solidly under him—keeps him isolated longer—reinforces his image of himself as withdrawn, frightened, and unlovable. After all, no one is trying to include him. It must be that no one wants to play with him.

We know that we must persist in including him. So we go after him and bring him into the group. However, for such a child we involve him in a special way that is responsive to his fears. We may need to be very gentle, and protective at first. We may pick him up and sit him in our lap or beside us, so he can feel we are going to take care of him. We can tell him that we will not let him get hurt, and he should tell us if he does. We should tell him we will help him play, that we want to play with him. And tell him that we are so glad he came to play with us.

> LEADER: OK, are we ready to start? Oh no! We have a problem. Sara didn't come with us. We can't start without her. Let me see what's wrong. Sara, come on, we need you to play with us.
>
> SARA: (She is sitting at a distance from the group, head lowered, not talking, not moving, not responding to your invitation.)
>
> LEADER: Well, we can't start without you. Here I come. (The leader gets up, goes over to Sara, and picks her up.) Hey, we want to play with you. You can sit with me. Here, you sit with me and we'll play together. Hey, now we can all play 'cause Sara is here! Now, let's sing our Hello Song to Sammy. (And she immediately starts the welcoming activity with Sara on her lap.)

NOTE: Whether Sara joins in with the singing is not important and should not be forced. In fact, she very likely will not join in yet. But that is OK. Just the fact that she is present, and feeling the group through you, gives her the opportunity to be involved. Not forcing her to **do something** will help build her trust in you. You are insisting on her presence, but you will give her some time to get comfortable. You do not want to put her on the spot right at first. So you have started your activity with the child next to you and you go around the circle. Sara will be the last child before you to get a turn. If she is still fearful of participating in the activity, you can do it as one — together.

Later on in the group, you are passing around nose wiggles. You might decide to give Sara the first wiggle, because, since she has stayed in your lap, you know she is beginning to trust you.

SARA: (She drops her head and hands and leans into you.)

LEADER: Hey, come back. We have to find a wiggle for Sammy. I'll help you. Hold my hand. (And you put Sara's hand on top of your hand. Then slowly, you move your hand, with Sara's on top, to Sammy's nose for a wiggle.) OK, Sammy, here we come. Hold on Sara. Don't let go. Here comes your wiggle, Sammy. (And Sara wiggles Sammy's nose through you.)

You have found a way for Sara to participate and to begin to reach out to others while being "protected" by you. This is a beginning.ea044

The child who shrinks from physical contact: This child truly seems afraid of touch. He is not empty and cold like the distant child, but seems to fear direct physical contact and closeness. It looks as though he thinks you are going to hurt him if you touch him, and so, **you** become afraid of doing just that. So he never gets touched in a sure, confident, pleasing way. He needs nurturing and safe playfulness. He does not need challenge or structure. Above all, he will need activities in which he can be touched and in turn touch others, in gentle, safe ways.

Hopefully, this child will be small enough for you to pick him up, baby style, and gently and soothingly bring him to your group.

Sticking Together During your Group

The issue of "sticking together" is not only pertinent to the starting of your group. It is a constant throughout the group. Sometimes, a child will attempt to change the activity:

LEADER: Tim, it's your turn. Give me a funny face.

TIM: Grrrrr!

LEADER: Wait a minute! That's a funny noise. We need a funny face. Do you have one?

TIM: Ai-Ai-Ai-Ai!

LEADER: Did you give me another funny noise? We're doing

faces, not noises. No fair doing another game! We need a face. Let's remind him what we're playing.

EVERYBODY: We're doing faces!

LEADER: (Using challenge and paradox). Now, I know Tim. He likes to play his own game instead of our game. I bet he's going to give us another noise. Let's see: Tim, we need a funny face.

TIM: (Puts his fingers in his ears and gives a funny face. He's not about to let us win a "bet!")

In this case, we did not even say, "Tim, you're not sticking together. You have to stick with the group and we're playing funny faces." Some leaders are explicit about verbally citing the "stick together" rule. However, as you can see, we can follow the rule implicitly. Whenever a child ventures away from the group or the activity, he is not sticking together and must be reinvolved in as playful and positive a way as possible.

Sometimes a child will try to involve another child in a private but disruptive and distracting activity or discussion. The children who do so are often the distant and seemingly disinterested children. An example follows:

John has turned to his neighbor, Fred, and they have started talking to each other and ignoring the activity that the rest of the group is involved in. It is not their turn. You could go on with the game, and not deal with them until it is their turn. But they are distancing themselves, and it is obvious to anyone who notices that they are not involved with the group. Letting it continue gives permission to distract and be distant. It tells the other children that what they are doing must not really be too important if you allow the two boys to have something better to do.

LEADER: Hold on. We have to stop for a minute. John, Fred. You're not with us. Are you playing your own game? You can't do that. You have to stay with us.

We can begin to see how children with different problems attempt to leave or change the group activity for different reasons. The children that you will have the most difficulty involving will be those who are emotionally distant and have never made attachments to their parents. They may need one-to-one therapy that will provide them with a chance to make an emotional attachment with **one** person. A group is a diluted situation which makes it easy for them to keep their distance. But if you have them in your group, do not give up. Keep them involved, but also see if you can refer them for individual therapy.

Now, we are going to be honest with you. In real life, children are sometimes excluded from Theraplay Groups. Some of the reasons are not in your control but some are. We will talk first about the ones that are in your control. Rubin had the experience of simply not being able to involve a tall, withdrawn fourteen year old boy. He obviously could not be picked up anymore. Persistent attempts and all the techniques she could think of did not work. She finally had to choose between persisting and holding on dogmatically to the stick together rule, or going ahead without the child. When all else fails, and you realize the group has been on hold for too long, as happened in this case, then go ahead without the child. However, do not go ahead without mentioning him and that he will be missed in the group. Also, if possible, have an adult stay with him until he can join the group again.

> LEADER: Oh dear! We really have a problem. Steve just won't join us today. We're really going to miss you, Steve. We wish you'd come play. We're going to get started; maybe you'll play with us later. Mrs. X, would you go sit with Steve and keep him company until he wants to join us?

Another example of a situation that is under your control is when a child demonstrates excessive difficulty with an activity, or with participating in the group on that day. There will be times when a child needs to "act out." He becomes highly disruptive and cannot be structured in the group. You have tried having yourself or another adult sit by him and help him participate, but this is not successful. You are taking up too much time trying to contain him, and you, the child, and the group are becoming more and more anxious. This child needs time **away**, but not **alone.** Tell him and the group that he does not seem ready to play, and have another adult take him to a different spot in the room and stay with him. She may have to hold onto him, structuring and nurturing, if he was explosively acting out. But if he was just being disruptive and distracting, then they can sit at some distance from the group, watching the rest of the activities. Always express your sadness that he cannot participate in the game—**but not disappointment at his behavior.**

A child's behavior is there for a reason. As an example, let us discuss acting out behavior. If there is any child that we would be brave enough to **predict** will act out some time during your group, it would be the abused child. We have found abused children to consistently have great difficulty with the closeness and support of a Theraplay Group. They have associated attachment and relating to being hurt. After all, they attached to their mother or father, and what did they get from that relationship? Abuse. Neglect. Being in close proximity to others, in a nurturing environment that is moving them ever more closely to trusting others, causes them to want (need) to **run.**

This urge to run is basically for their own protection. They are running away from getting close enough to be hurt. But they probably will not out-and-out run. Instead, they will become fidgety, they may talk too much, they will not be able to keep their attention on the activity or be able to take turns. They may attempt to hurt someone else or themselves. This child, contrary to any other type of child, needs some space and some separation. Being close terrifies him. In fact, with this child, giving him some space—but not too much—can help him develop the trust that **you** will not hurt him. To say this in a slightly different way, giving **this** child a little space when he is terrified might help him develop trust. But giving him space does not mean isolating him. That would verify his feeling that being with someone is bad. Instead, you can allow him to move away from the group **with another adult.**

Again, always have this decision in your control:

> LEADER (to the co-leader): Mrs. Carr, Johnny needs help. He's having a real hard time today. Why don't you take him over there and sit with him awhile until he feels better. And when he feels better, he can come back and play.

NOTE: Now, Johnny usually does not want to leave. **He is not acting out because he wants to leave.** And thus, he will put up some resistance to being removed from the group. So be prepared for this. In fact, he might say he does not want to leave, that he wants to stay. And this is really true: he **does** want to stay. But he **needs** to have some room right now. And **you** know it. Once again, and we cannot say this too many times, his behavior is telling you he needs room, although his words say something else. You understand his anxious behavior, and take steps so he can have the space that he needs for as long as he needs it.

> JOHNNY: No. No. I wanna stay. (He wiggles, and fights Mrs. Carr. She picks him up as best she can, containing his

arms, and takes him to the other side of the room where she sits him down, sitting down herself next to him with a hand on him in case he needs to be contained.)

MRS. CARR: Johnny, I'm going to stay with you until you feel better. It's OK. Here, you can hold my hand, I'll keep you company.

LEADER: (to the group) Mrs. Carr is going to take care of Johnny. She's going to help him so he feels better. Maybe later he can come back to play.

NOTE: This is very important for the leader to tell the group. They need assurances that Johnny is not being punished for his behavior and that you still want him back. They now know that, should they be in a crisis, you will respond to them and they will not be left alone.

Usually when a child is excluded, like Johnny, the leader talks to him from her position in the group. She might say, "Johnny, we hope you feel better so you can come back to play later." However, it may be better for your co-leader to give him reassuring and accepting messages than for you to call to him across the room. For Johnny's support to be effective, it should be close by and readily accessible. You must now be available to your group and entrust Johnny to his helping adult.

Rubin had a number of experiences in which the classroom teacher felt a child should be removed from the group. Trying to help the child participate was taking up too much of the group time. Reluctantly, Rubin would bow to the teacher's judgment concerning how to handle the child. After all, the teacher had him all day and knew more about him than Rubin did. When this situation does occur, it should be handled as much as possible like the previous cases described.

LEADER: We're having trouble getting started playing our game. Fred, I think you're going to have to sit over there while we play. I wish you could play with us, but you're not ready right now. We really want to play this game. Maybe you can play with us later.

NOTE: Always place Fred where he can watch the group. The point is not to punish him, but to allow the group to go on. Assuming you have an assistant, always send her to sit with Fred. She should also watch the group, and might comment on how much fun that game looks. With

Fred, make sure that his return to the group is under your control. He cannot say, "I'm ready. I want to come back." Either you, or your co-leader who is with him, should decide when he looks ready to participate.

> LEADER: (After the game is finished:) OK. Let's see if Fred is ready to come back with us. Let's see. (Checking him by looking at him) You look better. Maybe you're ready. I think you are ready to play. Come on back and sit right there. I'm so glad you're feeling better. Now everybody can play.

Now to talk about those situations that might occur that are not in your control. The older the children get, the more chance there is that you will run into these interferences. These situations are absences, mainstreaming, and punishments.

Absences: Never ignore when someone is absent. It should be brought up during the very first welcoming activity, when there is a time to greet each child.

> LEADER: Mary isn't here today? Well, next time, we're going to have to check her and make sure she's OK. We're going to miss her.

Next time, when Mary is back, special mention should be made that you all missed her last week and you are glad she is here today. Children who have been absent should get extra special nurturing on their first day back. This is taken directly from individual Theraplay when, on a child's first session after an illness, you always do primarily nurturing activities, even though, before he got sick you may have been focusing on challenge. An illness is a set-back. During illness you are less able to function and need someone to nurture you. Absences, even for reasons other than illness, can cause a child to wonder if he was missed. You can both recognize the returning child's need for a warm welcome back, and at the same time give him permission to "regress" by doing a few nurturing things with him at the beginning of his returning session:

1. If the child was sick, and you know or can find out what the illness was, lotion (powder, blow on) the appropriate body part. For example, if Mary had a cold, you can lotion her nose; if she had a sore throat, lotion her neck.
2. You can welcome the returning child by rechecking the basic body

parts you have played with before in the Theraplay Group sessions (nose, fingers, ears, etc.).

LEADER: OK, Mary's turn for our Hello song. Remember, Mary wasn't here last week. I'm so glad you're back. We missed you. Let's see if she brought everything with her so she can play. Well, your nose still wiggles, your eyes are still blue, and you still have your strong muscles. Good! OK, everybody ready to sing a special Hello to Mary 'cause we didn't get to sing to her last week.

Mainstreaming and other outside activities: Scheduling a Theraplay Group can be complicated, and it is even more so when different children are scheduled to leave your classroom at different times. Sometimes there may be strains on your priorities, and although you know all your children should be included in your Theraplay Group, either you have decided that this child needs more to be somewhere else, or you have been told that this child must be somewhere else at the time that your Theraplay Group is scheduled. Children going in and out of your group will have an effect on it. Not only will it distract the group, but it will be telling the remaining children that the group is not as important as what the other children are doing. If your group is a positive experience for the children, it is also telling them that, were they to have other pressures and expectations on them, they, too, would be expected to give up the group. This will bring a certain amount of insecurity into your group and you should be aware of this. This means that you may not be able to accomplish all you had hoped for in this group. It also means that you must take some steps to help the leaving or returning children as well as the remaining children with this disruption and loss.

Some suggestions:

1. When a child must leave, or when he comes back, formal good-byes or hellos are in order. If a child leaves, he will be highly aware of what he will miss, and that he is being taken away from something. It may be possible for you to tell him that you will "save" something from the group for him when he gets back. This can be a cotton ball that you were about to use to give nose tickles. Or maybe one remaining child can volunteer to play the next game with the leaving child during free time. If nothing else comes to mind,

reassure the child that you will save a treat for him. Then, remember to do it!

2. When a child returns in the middle of your group, stop the activity. Welcome him back:

> LEADER: Tom, you're back! Glad to see you! (and the leader shakes his hand in a welcome) We're playing _____. Let's tell Tom what we're doing. (And the leader sees if some of the children can tell Tom about the game.)

If there is too much leaving and returning, your group may need more nurturing than otherwise. Anything that causes a greater sense of insecurity in the group means that the children will need more nurturing. By definition, insecurity requires nurturing.

Punishments: Unfortunately, punishments periodically occur in school. In our experience, punishments often take the form of a child being excluded from something that he wanted to participate in. Therefore, two situations can occur.

Situation Number One: You are the classroom teacher leading your own group. A child has been "bad" and he is presently being punished in the room (i.e., finishing homework). It is time for your group. Since he is being punished and excluded from other classroom activities while completing his work, you are about to exclude him from the Theraplay Group. Seems logical. To do otherwise would seem as though you were letting up on his punishment. If you feel this way, you are thinking like a teacher is supposed to think. And the theory does seem logical: withhold something desirable from a misbehaving child so he will realize he should behave in order to get the desired thing. But think a little more. Yes, your Theraplay Group should be something desirable to the children in your class. But if that were all it was, it would simply be a tangible reward for good behavior (i.e.: Be good and you can participate in the Theraplay Group.) But your Theraplay Group is not just a desirable experience. It is a **needed** experience. There is a great difference between the two.

It is important that your children **want** to be in your Theraplay Group because **you** know that they are learning and growing and getting their needs met in the group. Therefore, the group should never be used as a reward for good behavior, nor should it be withheld if a child has been "bad" that day. Theraplay Group should always be a **required** activity. It should not be an experience that is left vulnerable to any behavior program you may have operating in your classroom. Think about this: There are children who have learned that they cannot have anything good. They punish themselves. They may, in fact, misbehave because they think that they do not deserve to have the pleasant experience of your Theraplay Group. Or, consider another situation. You may be really getting to a child's issues and he would rather not be in your group today, so he acts up because he knows you will punish him by excluding him and that is exactly what **he** wants. So, **always** follow the "stick together" rule. Remember you are doing a Theraplay Group because they need it just as they need reading or math. You would not exclude them from doing reading or math work, so do not exclude them from your Theraplay Group. If you find yourself wanting to exclude children, better ask yourself, "Why?"

Situation Number Two: You are leading your group, and a child is being extremely difficult today. You may be the teacher, leading your own group, or you may be a visiting leader with another teacher's class. You, or the teacher, have the same reaction that you might have if you were in a teaching situation: exclude the child as a punishment. He cannot be in your group if he continues to be "bad." Now, if all your children were supposed to be "good" in your Theraplay Group, what would you be doing the group for? Remember that you expect problems to surface; you **want** problems to surface. **This** is the place that you can allow the problems to come out. **This** is the place that you can help your children in very special ways that may not be possible at other times. If you do exclude him as a punishment, you are telling the other children to keep their problems hidden — to be "good." If that is really what you are after, then you are not running a Theraplay Group.

As you can see, these are problems you may face if you are the teacher leading your own group, or a leader running a group in another teacher's room. But you are most likely to want in some way to "punish" difficult behavior when you are new to Theraplay, and attempting to learn how to lead a Theraplay Group. If you anticipate having this reaction, then you can plan to try some new responses if it occurs.

It is a most difficult concept to learn, allowing problems to occur, yet dealing with them in a non-punitive, accepting, and constructive manner. In a way, you allow problems to occur, yet you take steps to help the child come to a healthier way of interacting. You do this, not by punishing, but by meeting the child's underlying needs when his problems surface.

There are a wide variety of positive, esteem-building, accepting techniques for dealing with children's problems. These will be discussed more fully in Chapter 13. Even though the chapter is for social workers, we encourage you to read the section on the unique methods of positive structuring.

HAVE FUN

When we train new Theraplay Group leaders, we see that all the previous rules could be carried out in a rigid, stilted, un-Theraplay like manner. After all, teachers are always in charge of the class and make the rules and tell the children what to do. Certainly, children are not allowed to hurt each other in school. And, when there is an activity at hand, the children must participate: i.e., stick together. But there is one last rule which transforms a classroom activity into a Theraplay Group; which transforms an activity that the class **must** do, into an activity that the children **want** to do. This is the rule to "have fun."

What does that really mean? And why is it so important?

Having fun: Picture a mother having fun with her baby. What do you see? A dour-faced woman, tired, forcing her baby to play with a rattle? Well, that wasn't what you expected us to say, was it! Of course that is not our idea of a mother. (It could happen, but it is not what we picture, and it is not what we want for children.) What do we really picture? A woman whose face is bright with love and excitement. Her eyes are shining and fixed with delight on her child. She has a ready smile, her expressions are varied and somewhat exaggerated as she tries to mirror her baby's emotions. She's right down where her baby is, talking to him in a way that rivets his attention on her in fascination and love. Her attention is all for him, and his is all for her. Did we get it right this time? That's what you hope to see, isn't it? Listen to a mother talking:

MOTHER: Ohhh! The rattle fell down. Come back here, rattle! Here it is! Here comes that rattle! It's gonna get you! (Shaking the rattle a bit away from her baby to get his attention so he might try to reach for it.)

She is positive, optimistic, pleasant, exciting, FUN! There is no monotony about her. Rather, when her child sees her, he anticipates that he will feel wonderful, that his mother will feel wonderful playing with him, and they will both enjoy pleasurable, happy surprises together.

Let us do something we do not typically do and think about WHY is there fun and excitement in a mother/child relationship? What is it there for and what does it do? If we understand its importance, we will know why we must recapture it in ourselves and bring it to—and let it out in!—our Theraplay Group sessions.

To preface our discussion about "fun," we are first going to return to something we already talked about. In a general way, our Theraplay Group rules parallel the five elements of Theraplay therapy: "The adult is in charge" is **the adult is in charge**; "no hurts" is **nurturing**; "stick together" is **structure**. But "have fun" is actually several aspects of Theraplay. In fact, it permeates the entire "doing of something" that is done from a Theraplay perspective. "Have fun," first of all, is the **play** in Theraplay. It tells you that this type of therapy is characterized by play. "Having fun" also parallels **stimulation**. Picture that mother with her baby? Now remember what we said about stimulation in the chapter on The Theraplay Principle:

> When Mommy nibbles his feet, hides and surprises during peek-a-boo, when Daddy skillfully throws him in the air and catches him, the baby feels **excitement, pleasure** sometimes mixed with **anticipation** of the unknown, and **delight** that the world is still safe, plus **exciting and inviting. His self-esteem and confidence increase when he feels the pleasure the adults are getting from playing with him!** Through these activities with his loving parents, the child is shown that it is **OK to venture out, to explore the world, and to grow and try new things.**

Those emphasized words—are they in your picture? **Can you FEEL them?** Can you remember how it feels when you **FEEL** them? If you cannot feel them or remember how it felt, find a mother and her baby. They may be your relatives, friends, or neighbors. They may be people you see at the park or playground. Get some books about babies and the first few years of life from the library and look at the faces of those babies. Look at the parents. Now can you **FEEL** those words? If so, that is what you must bring to and recreate in your group. If you cannot feel them, you may need time and help to begin to **FEEL** those feelings yourself.

If you find as you read this, or as you begin to lead a group, that you are turned off by the thought of these feelings we are talking about now, you **may** not be the person who can or should lead a true Theraplay Group with all the playfulness that it means and needs. We say this cautiously, because this playfulness is something that we adults, and teachers especially, have learned to submerge rather than to use. We have learned that school and teaching is serious business; where is there a place for play in that? Thinking like adults, we have equated learning with seriousness, responsibility, and importance, and that it certainly is. But, for some reason we have, at the same time, equated play with frivolity, unimportance, and something you only do when you are not working! How sad!

If you feel this way, and playfulness is submerged in you, you can find it and use it in your teaching, but you will most likely need help to do this. Otherwise, you probably will not be successful at leading a Theraplay Group.

Well, if you have not heard these well-known words before, this is the place to hear them: for children, their play **is** their work. That means that they are learning from play; in fact, young children **must play to learn.** For them, play is not unimportant; it is necessary. Why? Because, to learn, you must be able to keep your attention on the subject. To keep your attention there, it helps if you are interested in the subject; it helps if you are curious about it—if it **stimulates** your curiosity. When this stimulation is present in children, or in adults, they begin learning on their own. Self-motivation, we call it. We **want** to do something that is interesting to us, that excites us, that makes us feel satisfied, competent, proud of ourselves. You know where that pleasure to learn came from? It came from play/work that was FUN. We do not seek to do things that are unpleasant and self-deprecating. We will be attracted to activities and projects from which we expect to feel productive and good.

Thus, mothers invite their babies to learn by playing with them **and having fun with their babies at the same time.** Picture that mother again. Look at her face. Isn't it inviting, exciting? Doesn't it make you want to do what she is doing? Doesn't it make you want to play with her? Even if the play is a little hard, a little challenging, even a little scary. Doing it with her, with someone who is right in there with you, who is optimistic, supportive, encouraging you, with you all the way, that is what makes the difference. That is what tells you that growth and learning is fun. She **shows** you it is fun. She **makes** it fun.

As you read this, you may have realized that this "fun" and pleasure does more than make learning fun for children. It creates relationships. Not only does it attract the baby's attention to what his mother is doing, it attracts his attention to his mother. The exciting, pleasurable, loving atmosphere she exudes attracts him like a magnet. His eyes light up as she approaches. He smiles in anticipation. She feels wonderful. We are repeating ourselves, but for a reason. Just think what each of these people mean to each other; what they would do **for** each other. Well, it is easy to answer if we think about the mother: she would give her life for her child, probably. But routinely, she gives her time, her love, her dinner, her thoughts to her child. But her child does not do anything, does he? He just takes. No, he does not. He gives up being a baby. He learns. He tries. He speaks. He walks. He uses a fork, instead of his fingers. He becomes able to say good-bye to her because he knows she will come back. Rather than stay safe with her, and have all his needs met by her, he grows and becomes competent and confident in himself because **she** has had confidence in him. And, when he is ready, he leaves her.

A more powerful, empowering relationship can rarely be recreated anywhere else than between parent and child. However, if we want, we can take those elements that create that relationship and develop the best, most constructive teacher/student relationship possible—a relationship in which your troubled children will seek to participate in activities **with you** that will promote their growth.

Now, how do all those big ideas about mothers and babies and powerful relationships translate into what FUN does for your Theraplay Group? Just like mothers, you will exude the atmosphere of fun and playfulness to your class during your group time. You will let the seriousness of teaching fall away from you as you relax and lighten the mood for your group. You will sit on the floor with the children and sigh in pleasant anticipation of this chance to relax and have some "pure fun" with these children with whom you spend so much time. What a relief to put the pressures aside for a time, knowing that, as all of you simply enjoy this time together, your children are developing in incredibly important areas such as self-esteem, social awareness, caring for others, confidence!

You will smile. You will squeeze your neighboring child in a warm hello. Your eyes will twinkle as you get ready to surprise them with a new game, or challenge them with a twist of an old game. Problems do not defeat you, as they might in the role of a teacher. And you do not need to defeat the problem child either. You can use play to reach and involve him.

JIMMY: (He has come to the group and is sitting on his hands while the children, one-by-one, are passing around a hello with a handshake, and a greeting. It is his turn to get greeted and he is going to quash your game and composure by ignoring the game and continuing to sit on his hands.)

LEADER: Oh no! Jimmy, where are your hands? Oh, we have to find them. Are they in here? (and she begins looking in a variety of funny places like in Jimmy's shoe, Joey's hair, etc.) No. That's not Jimmy's hands. We've got to find them. Hey, did you leave them home? You can't do that! You have to bring them to group 'cause we always need hands to play with.

NOTE: There are any number of ways this leader can handle this playfully, and if one way does not work, she can try another. One way:

LEADER: Oh. There they are. You're sitting on them. Ha! And they won't come out? I bet they are stuck. You didn't put glue on them, did you? Then they won't come out. Oh dear. I don't think you'll be able to get them out 'cause you have to be real strong. (And with that temptation, Jimmy pulls out his hands.)

Another way:

LEADER: They're gone. Oh, what are we going to do? 'Cause you have to have your "hello" today. Oh, you **did** bring something for a hello. Tina, give the hello to his ears. Now don't leave your ears home next time, Jimmy.

Another way:

LEADER: (looking for Jimmy's hands in funny places) Ah! I found them! (Finding Jimmy's ears, feet, etc.) Hello, hands! (If Jimmy is ready to be playful, he just might, at this point pull out his hands to refute you, saying:

JIMMY: No! Here they are! (and you've got him!)

What a welcome change from the normal school routine! It's play! It's pleasurable! It's surprising! We feel good! And thus are the children drawn into the warm, accepting, and fun group you have created, and in doing so, they will face issues and will develop in areas that they otherwise might have avoided.

How to "HAVE FUN"

How do you, an adult teacher, capture the quality of fun with your class?

First, you must stop being a "teacher." You can, and should, still be a leader, but, at the same time, you are part friend, part mother or father, part playmate. It might help to think of yourself as the person who is responsible for the games, the decisions, being responsive to the children, **giving** to the children, making sure everyone is safe and participating. BUT after that, you are a playmate. Although you are responsible for the group, you can join in the fun at the same time. This may sound easy, but it is usually hard to do in practice, especially when you are learning. But, rest assured, it is do-able.

Second, YOU must have fun with what you are doing. Do not bring an activity that has no appeal for you. And, if you begin an activity, and YOU are not having fun, stop it. There may be some of you who are able to have fun with any activity. There may be some of you who are more particular about the activity. But be prepared for the day when YOU do not particularly feel like playing this particular game. You begin it, and DUD! It doesn't grab you. Well, if it does not grab you, how in the world are you going to grab the children with it? We all have our days, and when that happens, and you are not ready or able to have fun in a certain way, drop that game, and switch to an activity that fits your mood.

Here are some of the aspects of having fun, that were discussed by trainees as they struggled with the quality of bringing fun to their groups.

1. LET YOURSELF GO!
2. Having fun is being spontaneous.
3. It is being faster paced than you typically are.
4. It is being excited, yet it is being relaxed.
5. It is being "silly."
6. It is being in charge yet at the same time being a participant, joining right in with the children and enjoying the group **yourself**.
7. It is feeling comfortable with intimacy and play.
8. It is going back to how you felt as a kid yourself, playing with exuberance, excitement, and with little inhibition.
9. It is being playful.
10. It is having a twinkle in your eye.
11. It is being unpredictable.

12. It is saying to yourself, this group is going to feel totally different from school. This will be a pleasant haven for all of us to relax and let go of the controls that we must have to be students. Now we can be people, friends, playmates. Let's just enjoy each other!

There is nothing routine about having fun. Fun means surprises and the excitement you feel when you do not know what is going to happen but you are looking very much forward to it. That kind of anticipation of the unknown is very pleasant, stirs up interest, keeps people involved. It is not the same as fear of the unknown, because in that case, you sense discomfort and an unpleasant outcome. Anticipation of the **inviting** unknown is what keeps us going, and that is what you want to create in your children to keep them involved with the group.

So: You will never (or rarely and only for good reason) do the same thing twice. You may repeat the same **type** of activity (and this is common), but then you must create some pleasant change in it any way you can. It can be subtle (the words that you or the children have to say can vary), or the change can be obvious. It really is not important how great the change is, but just that it is present. Thus, the children can never predict just what you will do, or how they will have to play this game. Thus, they cannot run the group either!

Remember, things that become monotonous and predictable are dull and uninteresting. If you know just what is going to happen, you can, and will eventually, stop paying attention. Why listen when you know what the other person is going to say? In more formal phrasing, children maintain attention when the stimulus is appropriate to their level and its presentation is varied just enough each time to keep their attention rather than lose it. This is exactly what the aspect of "fun" is for.

So: You can play just like a kid. You can be silly. You can be mischievous. You can sit right down with them at their level and enjoy the play they give back to you when it is your turn to get a tickle or a treat. YOU can have fun.

We get this question often: "What if a child doesn't think the activity we brought is fun? What do we do then?" Horrors! Your worst fear has come true! A child has rejected this wonderful game you brought him. What do you do now? Try another game and see if he likes it, or let him sulk while the others play?

Neither!

If you let him sulk, you are giving him permission to withdraw and not stick together. If you try another game, you are agreeing with him that the game is not fun, and you are going to attempt to satisfy him by abandoning your game for another that he **might** like. And what if he does not like the next one? Can you see yourself, standing on your head as it were (I often think of it that way, when I feel this starting to happen to me), trying game after game, the child laughing inside over how he has gotten you so anxious about pleasing him? Boy, is he in control!

YOU can decide that a game is not really fun after all, or that this is not the right day for this game. But you will not decide it because a child happens to say, "This isn't any fun." This is an expressed wish to make you anxious. This does not tell you what he **needs**. You know what he needs. He needs to join in and be involved, and to have fun, and get nurtured and all the other wonderful things that will happen in your Theraplay Group.

You can handle this in a variety of different Theraplay ways. But before we look at some possibilities, there is one more important point to make. Children like the child described above, who chronically complain about your activities, will most likely be older, around eight years and above. They have learned that when they complain, and because they are older and we feel we must respect their opinion, they are able to get out of doing what they complained about. This is one type of situation that could happen in your Theraplay Group.

However, if a game is truly not fun, probably no one will actually **say** that. Instead, you will begin to see the signs, in the children, and maybe in yourself. Once again, in a Theraplay Group, you will be attuned to what is happening, to affect, to expressions, to feelings, rather than to what might actually be said. If there is no fun, the children will not be "with you." They might look sad because this activity is not meeting their needs. (They cannot tell you this; you have to be able to read it.) If you are not having fun, you may feel as though you are acting, or that you are just going through the motions of leading this group, but your heart is not in it. You may become easily irritated at the children's responses. But you are not having fun and neither are the children. They do not have to say it. You know. Now you must switch the activity.

LEADER: Boy! This isn't any fun! Let's do something else.

Now, how to use the rule of "Have Fun" to involve children in your group:

If a child does say, "This isn't any fun," you can do something that does not often happen in school: Agree with them! Adults are always trying to talk children out of how they feel. Children often hear: "Oh, don't say that! You really want to play with us, I know you do." If you argue with them, you are bound to continue their resistance, which of course, is what they want. This way they can use **your** insensitivity as a reason to be uninvolved with the group. Surprise them by agreeing that fun is important. And after you validate them, involve them in the solution:

JIM: This is boring. It's a baby game. I'm not going to play.

LEADER: Wait a minute, everybody, Jim thinks this is boring. We don't want him to be bored, 'cause that's no fun. Jim, tell you what. We're going to start this game and try it out. Now, you have to play with us. Then, after we do it once, let's see how we like it. Maybe you (or we) can figure out a way to make it fun. I (we) don't want to play it if it's not fun either!

(Then, after a trial run, you can see how it felt to you and the group. If Jim still says he's bored:)

Hmm. That's interesting. I liked it, we all liked it but Jim is still bored. OK, how can we make it more exciting? What do you think, Jim?

And, if he comes up with something, you can see if everybody wants to try it that way. That challenges him, and if that is what he needs, then he may be likely to get involved again. Also, **you** can change the same game by adding more challenge, making it longer, harder, more exciting. You do not have to leave it up to Jim alone to think of how to make it more interesting.

Now that you know the theory behind Theraplay Groups, and how we create the Theraplay atmosphere, let us look at how this is applied to children with varying needs.

Chapter 6

PULLING "THEORY" AND
"PRACTICE" TOGETHER

We have pulled together the Theraplay philosophy (theory, if you
will), the Theraplay Group rules (or practice), and **the group**
—descriptions of children in our classrooms—and created the following
chart. Here you see how different children with varying needs are all
helped by experiencing the atmosphere and interactions that occur in
our Theraplay Groups. You can use this chart in a variety of ways. It is a
quick, visual picture of how Theraplay Groups work. It can remind you
of the Theraplay messages a specific child might need. You can also use
the last column to develop goals for the group and for individual children in your group. These goals will be met naturally when you create
the Theraplay atmosphere.

However, this chart is not an all-inclusive list of every personality or
behavior type you will see in your classroom over the years. In fact, you
may have more difficulty than ease in deciding just which category
applies to which child. You may want to use different words, more
meaningful to you, to label the type of problems your children have. You
may need to create new categories. Feel free to mix and match categories.
Frequently, a child will have characteristics of more than one category.
Also, you may find that, when you first begin working with a child, you
think of him as having one type of problem. Yet, the more you work with
him, and as more behaviors or feelings emerge, or as you learn more
about his family, you come to realize that he has other needs, other
problems below the surface. Thus, you will begin to change both your
approach and the messages you give to him in your group.

This chart provides you with examples of types of children, and how
their needs can be met **automatically** in Theraplay Groups no matter
what their category might be.

The isolated child, in a world of his own, avoids eye contact and
connections with people. Thus he is out-of-touch with what is going on,

TABLE I
THE THERAPLAY GROUP MODEL

Observable Behavior	Type of Problem	Child's Unmet Needs	Meeting Needs in the Theraplay Group
Lacks eye contact Physically isolates self Does not initiate Unresponsive to others Ignores present reality	Isolated	Stimulation Involvement	
Clingy Excessive crying Difficulty separating Difficulty working independently	Overprotected Fearful	Stimulation Challenge Involvement	*THE ADULT IS IN CHARGE* Requires child to take role of child Provides structure Nurtures Maintains safety

Fears touch or physical
  closeness
Lacks eye contact
Excessive crying
Difficulty in tolerating
  change: attempts to
  control; rigidity
Ignores present reality
	Withdrawn
	Fearful
		Nurturing
		Structure
		Involvement
			"NO HURTS" Rule
			
			Creates atmosphere of safety and
			  nurturing
			Builds trust and caring
			Encourages acceptable alternatives to
			  aggression
			Encourages assertiveness

Never "gets enough"
Constantly demands
  attention
Seeks nurturing in
  inappropriate ways
Cannot share or take
  turns
	Needy	Nurturing
		Challenge
			"STICK TOGETHER" Rule
			
			Creates atmosphere of involvement
			  and caring
			Provides structure
			Keeps child involved with others
			
			"HAVE FUN" Rule

Avoids eye contact Lacks impulse control Easily overstimulated Short attention span	Impulsive Distractable	Structure Nurturing	Provides pleasure with others Provides incentive for staying involved Encourages expression of feelings Stimulates and excites
Provokes others Physical or verbally attacks others	Aggressive	Structure Nurturing	Helps child rise to challenge Provides playfulness

Attempts to control
  environment
Refuses nurturing
Assumes adult role by
  directing others
	"Little
	Adult"
		Adult in
		charge
		Stimulation
		Playfulness	

Refuses to accept
  responsibility for
  actions
Always changes subject
Attempts to control
Disruptive
May relate to people as
  objects
	Manipulative	Structure
		Nurturing
		Involvement	

is often unresponsive to others and what the group is doing. He needs **stimulation** and insistent **involvement** with others. He will get this automatically from the take-charge, involving adult, from being helped to stick together, and from the constantly inviting **fun.**

The overprotected and fearful child is not one who is fearful because of a history of lack of safety or caring when he was younger. This is the child who has been "over-babied" and not encouraged to venture out. He needs exciting **stimulation, challenge** to grow, and **involvement.** He will automatically be encouraged to assert because of "no hurts", will be involved with others through sticking together, and **fun** will stimulate, and excite him giving him confidence to rise to the challenge (i.e., to grow up!).

Other children who are withdrawn or fearful from family histories involving insecurity, neglect, or abuse, will primarily need **nurturing** and **involvement.** Since these children frequently have some aggressive behavior, they may need **structuring** also. In such cases, we take some unmet needs from more than one category on the chart. Such a child will be nurtured by the adult in charge who creates a safe, dependable environment, different than he is used to at home. Nurturing will also come from "no hurts," which insures that the atmosphere is conducive to building trust and caring between the group members who can serve as a healthier "family". He will also get structure from the adult in charge who will not allow things to become chaotic, negative, rejecting, or punishing. Sticking together also provides structure. Playfulness, positiveness, and protection will keep him involved with others.

The "needy" child is one who feels like a bottomless pit. You can never give him enough "mothering," nurturing. He may tend to cling to you, or cry when he needs more of you than you can give. He is truly like a baby, immaturely demanding all your attention, and being unable to share with others. To differentiate this child from the over-babied, withdrawn child, you will have to know something about this child's history and his present family situation. This child may have had a period of being neglected. Maybe he was pushed to grow up too fast. Maybe there was a time he was separated from his mother which caused him to regress and remain clingy (to her or to mother-substitutes, you!) for fear of losing her again. This child will obviously need as many **nurturing** and **attachment** experiences as you can provide. But along with that, to help him in social situations in which he may have to "fight" for attention, he would benefit from **challenge** in the form of learning to assert his needs with others. Thus, give him support, nurturing and special protection in your group. If necessary, keep him by your side to foster feelings of attachment. Your taking charge to assure that he is cared for, having the entire group be caring and nurturing via "no hurts," will create the safe, secure environment necessary for him to try other means of getting his needs met. With you and the supportive class by his side, he may eventually be encouraged (through modeling) to assert his needs in a more age-appropriate way rather than by clinging and crying.

The impulsive, distractible child may be the typical learning disabled child who truly cannot control his own attention. Although we realize much of this behavior is out of his control, we (adults) may have unwittingly given him the message that he is "bad," inappropriate, and can't he just pay attention? Over time, these children suffer from poor self-esteem because they cannot seem to satisfy the adult world. They get more criticism than praise.

Other children may be impulsive and distractible because of a lack of trust of others. They jump all around due to a basic anxiety over interacting with people. If they keep moving, they are not sitting targets. They will move before we can get to them, protecting themselves from the anticipated negative interaction.

Both types of children have difficulty making and keeping eye contact, lack impulse control, are easily over-stimulated, and have short attention spans for their age. They need gentle, accepting (not punishing, or repressive) **structuring**. The adult in charge will provide this in the Theraplay Group using all the positive, accepting methods of structuring that will be discussed further in Chapter 13. These children also need a great deal of **nurturing** to counteract the negative, critical messages they typically receive. They will especially need nurturing after a display of particularly impulsive or distractible behavior. Not only will they get this nurturing from the "no hurts" and "stick together" rules, but your **manner** of structuring will nurture also. The fact that your structuring is non-punitive, non-critical, and not repressive will, in itself, be a nurturing form of structuring. It is built naturally into the Theraplay approach.

Here comes the aggressive child. He may be "the bully" of the class: the "tough guy." Or he may be a child who functions well most of the time, but then unpredictably strikes out. Or he may appear appropriate on the surface, but as you watch carefully, you notice he might scratch his neighbor innocently, squeeze his hand too hard, or hug too tightly. These are signs of hidden aggression. The bully or tough guy does not hide it, but takes any opportunity to provoke fights, or to physically **or verbally** attack others. Just like the impulsive, distractible child discussed above, these openly aggressive children have received punishment in return for their aggressive behavior (aggression for aggression!), and repression. They need firm, positive **structure** and **nurturing**. Of course, these are carried out through the adult being in charge, and by maintaining safety.

The "little adult" is a grown-up little child, often very competent, verbal, wanting to help you and also help his peers with classroom tasks. Often we love this child because he is so helpful and no trouble. In fact, he may ride herd on other problem children in the class, serving almost as an aide to the teacher. This behavior, however welcomed, should alert you to this child's underlying needs. He has learned to be grown-up. He has been rewarded for being competent, composed, controlling, helpful **at the expense of being a child.** Once you see this, you may notice additional behaviors that are not necessarily so appealing and helpful.

For example, he may try to control his environment and even you. Since he has been rewarded for taking care of (controlling) children, he thinks he should do the same for adults. He may begin to tell you that it is time for such-and-such an activity. Now, if you have actually forgotten the time, you may at first welcome his reminder. But, next time, when you intentionally extend an activity, or change the order of the day, he is still reminding you and trying to structure you! However benign and helpful this behavior may appear, it signifies a "little adult," a child who has difficulty being a child, enjoying play, letting the adult be in control, letting down his guard, and being nurtured.

This child will be tough to reach, but more than anything, he needs the **play** in Theraplay. He needs the excitement, the exuberance, the spontaneity of Theraplay. And he needs **you** to be in control so he can relax his vigilance and enjoy interactions with others. Your being in charge and giving him experiences of "having pure fun" will be what he needs from your group.

Last, but certainly not least, is the manipulative child. He will tax your patience because he has learned to be persistent and creative in running people around in circles. He is the "what-did-I-do?" kid who innocently resists accepting responsibility for his actions. He may flit from subject to subject, hoping to get us off balance by making us chase after him. He tends to be disruptive to the group and the activity, and may try to sabotage games, hoping to ruin things for others and wind up as the mischievous culprit. "Ha, ha! Look what I did!"

You know the messages he has received from the world. Exasperation from adults, perhaps even rejection when they begin to stay away from him. Since people tend to avoid him, including his parents (let's keep peace by leaving him alone rather than trying to deal with him), he has not received the necessary structure that would keep him with others. If he has received any structure, it was as a last resort and probably quite punishing. Like the impulsive and distractible child, he has a negative, "trouble-making" image of himself that he now perpetuates. How do you begin to reverse that?

This child needs **very** firm **structure,** the accepting **nurturing,** and the insistent **involvement** of the Theraplay Group. Not only the adult being in charge, but the entire group can provide the structure because, above all, this child really does NOT want to be excluded. He wants to stay in the group in order to manipulate it. But if the adult guides the group into structuring this child, reminding him to "stick together," to "stay with us," showing him that they want him involved and included, that they accept him, manipulation and all, he will come around and increasingly respond to the group activity. He will respond because he will be getting acceptance and nurturing rather than repulsion and punishment. And it was acceptance and nurturing that he needed in the first place, even though he developed behaviors that got him repulsion and punishment instead. In the Theraplay Group, you can reverse this negative cycle.

We hope this helps you see how this all fits together. But only in the doing will you really understand how this works.

Chapter 7

THE RITUALS OF A THERAPLAY GROUP

The beginning and the end of your group sessions mark special times of saying hello and saying good-bye. There are a variety of ways that you can do this, and yet, there are two uniquely Theraplay activities that epitomize the nurturing aspect of Theraplay and that, therefore, establish an atmosphere of deliberate caring from the beginning to the end of each session. These two activities, are Check-Ups and Food Share.

Now, as we said when talking about "fun," even though you may use these activities each time you have your group, you will want to vary, however slightly, the way you do them each time. This keeps the children stimulated and interested. However, these experiences have the potential for becoming very important to your group and to the children in it. Although the word "rituals" may imply a repeated, predictable, unvarying routine, we use it here to mean a particular type of activity that the children can count on to provide them with nurturing, acceptance, and even a little indulgence. These are the good "rituals" of a Theraplay Group.

These two activities did not start out as rituals when Theraplay Groups were first tried in classrooms. Rubin took them directly from the group of typical beginning and ending activities frequently used in individual Theraplay therapy. But as more and more people began to lead groups, and we saw how a wide variety of children responded to these groups, our social worker colleague, Diane Mirabito, began to realize that these two activities became important symbols to the children and also contributed to the group's development. Later, when more leaders were trained, we found that these activities were also important to the leaders! Let us take a look at what these activities can mean to the children and to the leaders of the group, and how they help create the Theraplay atmosphere and foster group development.

CHECK–UPS

Check-Ups is a perfect way to say hello, check on the status of each child, and to nurture everyone. The leader begins by acknowledging the presence of the child next to her. "Jimmy, let's see how you are today. Well, you brought your eyes, and they are still blue. Good! And your ears are still wiggly. And, did you bring all your fingers? Yup. And your muscles? Thank goodness, cause we're going to need them. And you look all ready to play. Great!"

Check-Ups gives each child a moment in the spotlight, acknowledges that he is still the child of last week, that he still has all those fun things that he had before, welcomes him back, and gets him ready for fun. During this time, the group can sing a special song to each child, they can all give him a rub, handshake, hug, etc.

Check-Ups often becomes more than a simple acknowledgement of the child's presence in the group. It becomes a powerful vehicle for nurturing. This is how it happens.

As you are checking a child, you see a hurt (on his hand, arm, face, etc.). "Uh, oh. I see a hurt, Susie. Oh dear, hurts are yucky. You can't play if you have a hurt. We have to fix it." (And you reach for the lotion, carefully rubbing a little all around the hurt. As the group develops, each child can lotion the hurts of the child next to him as the others watch each child have his turn.)

It will not take long before the children will begin to expect you to lotion their hurts, and, should you try to skip this activity, hoping the group is beyond needing this, you will find that a child says, "Hey, you didn't lotion hurts!" or "Look, I have a hurt." Or, more interesting yet, the children will tolerate your trying a new activity, but, sometime in the middle of your group, Johnny will turn to you and say, "Look, I have a hurt." He is telling you that he still needs deliberate nurturing, that this is one place he does not have to be a "big boy" and tolerate his hurts, that having this time means a great deal to him and he is not yet ready to give it up, as you had hoped.

Where else in school can a child get cared for so obviously and totally? When is there ever time to notice those little signs which are hints that a child is troubled or feeling discomfort, or even actually hurt? Attending to hurts at the beginning of your Theraplay Group will become a "sure thing"; an experience that they will come to count on; a time that they will be nurtured without having to ask for it. If you add up all those aspects of Check-Ups, they spell SECURITY.

FOOD SHARE

There are many groups that enjoy a treat together at the end of their session. But there is no other group of which we are aware that carries this out in such a deliberately nurturing (even regressive) way. The Theraplay activity of Food Share embodies this concept. In this closing activity, the leader begins, holding the treat (small pretzel, raisin, piece of cookie, etc.) in her hand, turning to the child next to her, and **feeding** the treat to the child. Now, when you look at the description of this activity in the back of this book, you will see that all types of variations can be done. You can even give verbal messages about the group or about each child along with the treats if you wish. But the greatest value of this activity is in the regressive **feeding**. A mother **feeds** her baby. This signifies not only the baby's dependence on his mother, but his **trust** in her as well. He opens his mouth and lets her put something in it. Trust and dependence are related. You must trust someone before you are willing to reveal any dependence (interdependence is a better word) or vulnerability.

Thus, in Food Share, we never let the child feed himself. (But never regard "never" as absolute. Depending on the stage of the development of the group and the ages of the children in the group, we sometimes have allowed children to feed themselves.) And you will get some children who have great difficulty with being fed, no matter what their age. We have had some pre-schoolers who look away, lower their eyes, and cannot open their mouths if someone else is holding the food. They might open their mouths up until the last second, and then their hand comes up to put the food in their mouths.

Now, should this happen to you, you may find yourself tempted to say, "OK, Kathy, you watch while I give Tony his treat and you'll see it's OK." In fact, you may want to say this type of thing in other situations when one child has difficulty with an activity in the group. It sounds logical, too. Watch someone else do it who does not have an issue with it and you will see it is not something to be afraid of. If he can do it, try to swallow your fear and be like him. Can you see how this way of helping children does not usually help? Watching someone else do something does not help **this** child with **his** problem. In fact, pointing this out to him might make him feel worse. "He can do it, why can't you? See, it's 'silly' to be afraid." Implying these messages means you are ignoring the child's feelings. However safe it may be for others, **this** child is afraid. His fears need to be acknowledged.

Now, to get back to the child who is having difficulty, let us take a closer look at all the nuances that comprise Food Share so we can understand why it is so important and why it can be so difficult.

Food Share is very **intimate.** After all, you are not a baby, and you are letting another person feed you, put food in your mouth with their fingers. It is intimate from both sides, also. Some children have difficulty feeding others. Getting one's fingers near, or possibly in, another's mouth is just too close. This is part of the regressive aspect of Food Share. Fingers in mouths.

Food Share is **fun.** We're going to have fun like kids, not grown-ups. We're going to eat with our fingers and hands and have fun with food. (Can we ever do that? Only in other intimate situations, a la Tom Jones, or when we were babies.)

Food Share is **direct** and **deliberate.** Each person faces the other. Making eye contact is natural in this position, yet it can feel embarrassing, it feels so close and intimate. Some children, and many adults, want to look down or away, not wanting to face the person who is getting so "personal." And there is no distraction, no facade to what is happening. One person is being fed by the other. There is no way to kid yourself that this is something else.

Food Share is **indulgent.** One is treated to food. For children who deny things to themselves, this can be difficult for them. They, in fact, may reject the treat, saying they do not want any or they do not like it.

In Food Share, one person must allow another to take complete care of him. The child being fed is completely in the role of the child. He is not in control. He must feel OK about the other's being in control. He is wholly "dependent." This is extremely difficult for the children who are competent and independent, so much so that experiencing their dependence (remember, they are still only children) makes them anxious and uncomfortable.

For children, and adults, who have problems with intimacy, regression, fun, directness, dependency, or indulgence, Food Share will be a place in which these conflicts will surface.

THE IMPORTANCE OF THESE RITUALS TO THE GROUP

When Check-Ups and Food Share are repeated in session after session, they begin to stand for the unique messages that Theraplay gives: unconditional caring, and to be cared for even in the face of rejection. Because of this, they become increasingly important to your group. As Diane Mirabito so ably put it, these activities are concrete demonstrations of mutual caring. We do not talk about it, we **do** it. What more obvious way to demonstrate caring than to "make hurts better" and to feed each other? The fact that the children ask for these activities and remind you when you have forgotten them attests to their **need** for them. They will come to count on these two activities as a time when they will be recognized and nurtured regardless of whether or not they are able to express these needs.

Repeating these activities, even though you will modify them each time or often, will reassure your group that you recognize their need for these experiences and will provide them as long as they need them, no questions asked. In a group using Theraplay, in which there are always changes and surprises such that the group can never predict what is going to happen, some stability—not boredom, but stability—serves an important purpose. It anchors the group with secure experiences at the start and end of the group. As the children feel more and more secure, they will develop increased trust in those who are making the group secure. That will first be you, and then this will transfer to the other children in the group, since they will be more and more involved in the check-ups and food share as the group develops over time.

Security and trust—two basic foundations on which your group is based. Without them, the children will not grow from within.

THE IMPORTANCE OF THESE RITUALS TO THE LEADER

Not only will Check-Ups and Food Share become important to your group, but they will become important to you also. Although these activities always meant a great deal to us, we never thought too much about their value until we began watching trainees learn to lead Theraplay Groups. We noticed that both activities became rituals for the trainees as well as for their groups. We would guess that this happened for very similar reasons as for the children.

First of all, when faced with leading a group that had to be lively, interesting, exciting, surprising, and in which activities should not be repeated, these were two exceptions to that rule, two activities that the **leaders** could count on to be available to them, to return to, to address the needs of all those involved without the leaders having to think too much about why this particular activity was needed. Check-Ups gave them a place to start, a way to set the atmosphere, a way to differentiate the group from what had come before. Food Share gave them a relaxed, unpressured, fun way to end the group, again in a manner that differentiated the group from the typical classroom routine, for them as well as for their children. It allowed the teachers to **have some fun!** What a pleasant relief for all! Even though leading a Theraplay Group can be difficult what with having to be on your toes at all times, these rituals seemed to help our trainees relax and have fun with their groups.

We each remember times when we would try to omit Check-Ups, or try to hurry through it, not lotioning each child. It did not feel right. We felt that we were depriving the children of something that they needed that was very important **to them** — a close, sincerely caring look at themselves. Just because **we** thought we should have more time to do some other types of activities, we would try, usually unsuccessfully, to shorten the time for Check-Ups. Our groups let us know that we had not met **their** needs.

Thus these two rituals will become signals to the children and to yourself that roles are being switched, the experience of school will be different, needs will be met, fun will be had. This is a Theraplay Group!

Chapter 8

THE STRUCTURE OF THE SESSION

PART I: SPECIFICS FOR INDIVIDUAL SESSIONS

An important thing to remember about using Theraplay Groups is that the specific techniques are easily adaptable to your needs. The following ideas on how to structure Theraplay Group sessions are given as guides; many of the suggestions that we make from our experience can be adjusted to fit your situation.

Where to Have your Group

Think carefully about the best location for your Theraplay Group. It is important to choose one specific physical space. Having a place that you and the children can count on makes it more consistent, easier on all of you, and eliminates last-minute problems. The space should of course be large enough to hold the whole group comfortably and small enough to be cozy. We would never, for instance, try to hold a Theraplay Group in a corner of the gym: such a large space is too undefined. The ideal location is a corner of the classroom, with low partitions (such as cupboards or shelves) on the third side. The sense of being semi-enclosed helps give structure, aids in control, cuts down on distractions, and adds to a feeling of coziness. Be careful, though. We once made the mistake of setting up next to the toy shelf! We had to do some rearranging before the next session!

We do our groups with everyone sitting in a circle (or a semblance thereof) on a rug (or mats), in a designated corner of the room, thus doing away with the props of teaching. One large rug is definitely preferable to individual carpet squares. In fact, we often find carpet squares or individual mats very tempting for the children to play with or move around. We have seen groups where each child had an individual carpet square, and it appeared to foster a sense of separateness which we generally do not want to encourage in the Theraplay Group. We feel that

67

having the whole group on one rug facilitates the development of group cohesion. It emphasizes, without words, that we are a unit. However, there may be a child who, because he is very active or needs a great deal of external structure, may need to sit on a chair or on his own carpet square. Or you may have a room in which there is no rug, and in this case, you must provide something comfortable to sit on.

There are other unique situations that would call for a modification of the circle-on-the-rug format. If, for example, you were leading a classroom for the physically handicapped, there might be real problems in trying to have everyone on the floor. In such a case, it would be perfectly legitimate to arrange wheelchairs in a circle for your group. The important elements to retain are the defined space, the circle, and the closeness. A rule of thumb for the amount of space needed is: everyone sitting with legs folded, not "squished," but with knees touching, or almost touching. In one classroom where nearly all the children were extremely distractible and needed much structure, we suggested that everyone sit with "knees touching," with a long sheet wrapped around the outside of the group on everyone's shoulders, enclosing them in a sort of "tent." This provided the needed structure to keep the group together, as well as a very cozy feeling.

Materials

Theraplay uses very few props, but there are a few standard materials that we use and keep close at hand. Put these in a small box or bucket, store it on a shelf or in a closet, and bring it with you to the circle for each session. In the group, keep the box behind your back and bring out materials as needed. The basic materials are:

a shaker box of baby powder
a bottle of hand lotion
a soft foam rubber ball suitable for catching
a small baby blanket or large scarf
an edible, reasonably healthy treat (crackers, pretzels, raisins, cookies)

Useful materials to either keep on hand or bring in on occasion for specific activities include:

watercolor markers
cotton balls
feathers
masking tape

balloons
towels
aluminum foil (for making hand prints)
pillow
large newsprint or construction paper
crazy foam (foamy soap in an aerosol container)

When to Schedule your Group

When and how often to schedule a Theraplay Group is an individual decision. Sessions should be approximately 30 minutes long (but allow 45 minutes so you do not have to stop in the middle of a game). Your group should be held at least once per week, but depending on the needs of your classroom, you could schedule your group as often as once every day. Some teachers like to begin the day with a Theraplay Group, while others prefer the end of the day. Frequently, the choice of time is most influenced by external factors, such as when the children are mainstreamed to other classes, or when they leave the classroom to receive other services. Since all class members must be included, if at all possible, schedule accordingly.

Beginning your Group

At whatever time or day your Theraplay Group is scheduled, you will need to plan ways to lead your class into the group. Children may need to have some external structuring provided to help them with this transition, especially since the Theraplay Group may be quite different from the rest of the daily routine. It is best to make sure there is a definite break between the last activity and the Theraplay Group: i.e., have everyone at their desks before starting. You may think of ways to make the transition itself part of the fun of the group. For example, you can make a "snake" by collecting children one-by-one, all holding hands in a line as you move to the circle. Or you may go to the circle and call children one-by-one to join the group. It is often necessary to assign places, especially when you have identified those children who will need to sit next to an adult. If you do assign places, be sure to do it in a warm, nurturing manner: "Tommy! I have a special place for you right by me!"

We begin the first few sessions by going over the rules: No Hurts, Stick Together, and Have Fun (our favorite). We make sure the children understand what is meant by the rules, and that they remember them. Going over the rules serves two purposes: it familiarizes the children with the atmosphere and also provides additional structure. With young children (3 to 5 years old), we usually do not discuss the rules. We simply begin with getting-to-know-you activities and they learn the rules "by doing," by how **we** carry out the session.

The Sequence of the Session

Each Theraplay Group session has a clearly defined structure in itself, with a beginning, middle, and end. Activities chosen are appropriate to each section, as well as to the needs of the children. Beginning games involve greetings or "how are you" activities, generally contain a strong component of nurturing, and set the atmosphere of the group.

Since everyone must be relatively OK and ready to have fun, Check-Ups and taking care of any hurts are standard openings. Other typical activities are verbal greetings, smiles, handshakes, "eye-hellos," checking for hurts, saying what is special about each person, a "hello" song, etc. The common elements are the atmosphere of safety and nurturing, and the special acknowledgement of each person.

Middle activities are more active and involving. These games are most often characterized by, or can be used for, the elements of challenge and stimulation. This is the time that you pick an activity which addresses the needs of the whole group or a particular child. For example, Partner Pull-ups is a challenging game, and one that calls for cooperation. You might choose this game to involve a needy, demanding child who cannot share **anything.** It will challenge him to accomplish something through his own effort (instead of your giving it to him), and he will have to share the activity with another child. For the group, it is a graphic and unspoken demonstration of the value of cooperation. Beach Ball Name Game can be chosen to structure the impulsive, distractible child. He will have to pay attention in order to play. When the whole group needs to work on taking turns and cooperating, choose a game like Blindfold Friend Guess. This one gets everybody involved in the fun, and makes it easy to wait for a turn.

The ending section of a Theraplay Group is again quiet, calming, nurturing. We give a treat (Food Share), or a special good-bye ("I had fun with you today." "I liked the way you laughed today.")

Just as there was a clear beginning to your session, it is essential to provide a clearly defined end. When starting the last activity, it is helpful for the leader to announce, "This is the last game." When that game is over, you recap what happened, and mention that there will be more fun next time.

Then, just as you gradually put the group together, you carefully disband it. The children can be called one or two at a time to return to their seats. If your transitions do not need to be as structured as this, be sure that the adults are with the children as they leave the circle, extending the nurturing with a hand on a shoulder or a quiet comment.

Thus, the rhythm of each Theraplay Group is related to providing the four essential requirements for healthy development: Structure, Challenge, Stimulation, and Nurture. Structure and Nurturing are particularly emphasized in the beginning and end of each session, while Challenge and Stimulation fit naturally into the middle.

Planning your Session

The very essence of a Theraplay Group is spontaneity and playfulness. It may appear contradictory, but the only way to achieve this is through very careful planning and goal-setting. Only when you know where you are going, can you relax and enjoy the trip!

You will need to consider both long-term goals for the group and individual students, and short-term specific goals for each session (or a small group of sessions). Within that framework, you will need to find a balance between working on goals for individual children and goals for the group as a whole. Remember that since this is a group technique, the growth of the **group** is of primary importance and should be your major focus. In practice, it is amazing to discover that most individual needs are met through the involvement in the group process. By definition, a Theraplay Group geared toward the needs of the group will also meet many individual needs.

The kinds of goals you will set for your group will reflect the needs of your students, and will be compatible with both academic and social goals for your students. In Chapter 6, we discussed the goals that "come naturally" into a Theraplay Group. Here is another way of stating the goals you may have for your group.

Thus your individual goal for an impulsive, distractible child may be making eye contact with others. This, in turn, is incorporated into the group goal of taking turns. You will choose activities that meet needs for

FIGURE I

Examples of Theraplay Group Goals

LONG-TERM		SHORT-TERM	
Group	Individual	Group	Individual
cooperation	attention skills	taking turns	eye contact
	appropriate interaction		sharing

structure and nurturing (See page 56). In the game of "eye-hellos," children pass a greeting around the circle (taking turns) by a look and a smile or nod (requiring eye contact).

For the needy child who is constantly demanding and cannot share, your goal will be to increase appropriate interactions, beginning with being able to share. Again, this is integrated into the group goals of cooperation and taking turns. Nurturing and challenging activities (food share, passing along a lotion rub) will help meet both this child's needs and your goals for the group as a whole.

Often individual members of the group will have conflicting needs; e.g., one needs intensive nurturing, another needs challenge. You may handle this by picking one activity for nurturing and another for challenge. However, with many activities, a simple shift in the emphasis, or in the way YOU interact with a child during the session, will address these varying needs.

For example, Johnny is very manipulative and distractible. During Hand Letters, you hold his hand in yours while, with your other hand, you trace the lines in his palm to find the letter A. Your physical contact is structuring for him, helping him control his impulsivity. And who can be distracted when he is finding letters in his own hand? You have met his needs in a very nurturing way. When it is Mary's turn, she is fearful of physical contact and tries to control interactions, so she promptly finds her own "A." Laughing, you say, "Hey, that's my job!" and gently holding her hand, you are amazed to find—"Wow, here's an X!" Mary is involved in an interaction, even though she tried to avoid it, and she has been challenged to find a new letter instead of rigidly copying someone else. By changing the way in which you interact, you can use the same activity to meet differing needs.

Working with Others to Lead your Group

It is possible for just one adult to conduct a Theraplay Group. However, not only can this be a great strain on you, but subtle behaviors that signal a child's problem will be lost to you. Therefore, we strongly recommend that there should be at least two adults functioning as co-leaders. You might want even more adults if the group is made up of very young children or if the children have more severe emotional problems. Adults who would be likely co-leaders are teachers, aides, and social workers or counselors. Speech and language therapists interested in promoting pragmatically appropriate communication might be interested in supporting your Theraplay Group goals. It is essential that all the adults work together as a team to make the group function, and that all are involved in the sessions. One adult can pick up on what the other may miss. If a child is having problems, one adult can be available for special help. Having co-leaders also recreates the model of two parents working together.

Be sure to provide a time for co-leaders to plan ahead for sessions, to set goals together, and to "debrief" after a session. One of the things you must prepare for in your planning is what to do when something goes wrong in a session (and believe us, it will!).

Dealing with Problems

In our experience, problems most frequently occur during Theraplay Group sessions because the leaders have not provided enough structure. Sometimes the children become over-excited with an activity, or someone may get hurt, and the group no longer feels safe. If this happens, **STOP.** Stop the game, get everyone quietly settled in their places, and make sure the adults are in charge. Discuss briefly what happened:

    LEADER: We got too loud; it wasn't fun anymore.

or

    LEADER: Johnny got hurt and the rule is NO HURTS. Let's make sure Johnny is OK.

Then, **try the game again,** but slower and with more structure. This retry is very important because it reassures the children that we are taking care of them and that we **can** make this activity safe. We do not have to abandon the whole activity; we do not have to punish or threaten anyone; we do not have to exclude anyone; we do not have to deprive the group of this activity. Rather, WE take the necessary steps to make the activity do-able for this group at this particular time. In fact, a general rule of thumb is that whenever **you** are feeling uncomfortable with the way your group is responding to any activity, SLOW DOWN. This will make it easier for you to feel in charge and will make everyone feel safer.

For example, in a game of "Touch Blue," in which all the children simultaneously had to touch something blue on another child, we did not carry out the game with enough structure for this group to feel safe. Thus, we had a shrieking mass of children all "touching blue" at once and all over each other. Not surprisingly, there were several complaints and unhappy, anxious faces when everyone unraveled, and there was also one hurt.

We responded immediately by stopping the game and allowing everyone to settle into their places in the circle. Then we attended to the hurt. Lastly, we re-did the game, but added more structure without taking the fun out of it. This time, we went around the circle, one-by-one, touching blue on another person and not letting go until everyone was touching blue on someone else. This slowed the pace down substantially, made it possible for the leaders to provide more individual control if needed, and made the children feel more protected. The game ended positively and pleasantly, allowing the children to feel that they **could** complete an activity constructively and that their need for more structure did not destroy the activity.

Just think how guilty a child must feel when, in his need to explode or rush into action, he destroys an activity for his whole class. Rather than make him the cause of your giving up an activity, **you** must take the steps to help him participate in the activity. As you become more experienced, you will find that you are constantly modifying your activities or lesson plan, just as we did in this example, because you are responding to the needs of the moment.

After the session is over, and you conference with your co-leaders, you might hear different views on why the group or a child had difficulty with a certain activity, or with the session that day. It is important to take these ideas into account in planning subsequent sessions and in anticipating how you will handle the problem if it comes up again. The important thing to remember: plan ahead so that you are ready to respond.

Sometimes a child may be especially difficult and continually disrupt the session. One of the adults should give special attention to helping him remain with the group, or going with him, away from the group, if necessary. When he is in control again, the adult can help him return to the group. There is no punishment, and there are no reprimands. It is **critical** that one of the adults accompany the child if he must leave the group.

Sometimes there are a lot of problems and the session is just not working. In this case, stop the session. Say, "Oh dear, we're not having fun! No one's sticking together and we just can't have Group today. Maybe next time we can do it." **Be sure** to have a quiet nurturing ending to the session; it is needed now most of all.

One very important point: If any type of token economy, reward system, or behavior modification program is being used in the classroom, Theraplay Group sessions **must** be separate from these. Remember, in Theraplay Groups we **want** problems to surface so that they can be dealt with; we want spontaneity, we want growth from within—not "good behavior"—so we must not use behavior modification techniques during the group, nor should we either give or withhold tokens.

We have a really delightful example that illustrates why Theraplay Group sessions need to be a separate entity in the sense of no tokens or points. Tregay used a variety of techniques in her classroom including a token economy and behavior modification program. The children earned "points" for a variety of behaviors, one of which was following the teacher's directions. One day in Theraplay Group, they were passing around lotion rubs (a little dab of lotion rubbed on your neighbor's arm or elbow or ankle, etc.). It was Tregay's turn to get a rub from the child next to her. He was new to the class; a very angry and aggressive child who related to all adults primarily in negative, hostile ways. Gerry said, "Well, where shall I put the lotion?" And Tregay said, very dramatically, "Anywhere you want—EXCEPT—just DON'T—whatever you do!—DON'T put it on the end of my nose!" Of course, he immediately put it on the end of her nose, and the whole group fell over laughing! They had found an acceptable way for Gerry to "disobey the teacher," and it turned the tables on him by making it a positive interaction.

Thank goodness she did not have to withhold points, or "modify his behavior" to follow directions! This was a real turning point for Gerry as he began, with great difficulty and continued problems but also with great progress, to build a positive relationship with an adult. He absolutely loved the episode. It even became a "family joke" in the classroom and was frequently and successfully repeated in many later group sessions.

PART II: GROUP DEVELOPMENT OVER TIME

Like each individual Theraplay Group session (and like most groups of any kind), there is a definite rhythm to the development of the group over time. In our setting, we are talking about changes that occur across the school year. Group development closely parallels the sequence of a single session. You will need to start with nurturing. As the children begin to trust and feel safe, issues will begin showing up and sessions will become more challenging and stimulating. And as the year winds to a close, your group will need to end with a lot of quiet structure and nurturing as they deal with good-byes.

In the initial stage of the group, the adult leaders provide safety and caring for the children. The adult must insure the comfort and the sense of closeness, so that the children can begin to trust and to feel safe together. Therefore, your beginning group activities will be designed primarily to provide structure and nurturing. Such activities as Check-ups, Fixing Hurts, Lotion or Powder Rubs, and Food Share will be heavily used in the first months of your Theraplay Group. (In fact, we have occasionally found an extremely needy group that never really got past this stage during the entire year! In such a case, do not try to push the group, as they will not be able to move on until they have had enough of the nurturing that they need.)

One of our primary expectations when using Theraplay Groups is that the children will become more able to engage in positive interactions with others. In other words, they will become able to give to, as well as take from, others. However, since each child must first have some of his own needs met before he will be able to give to others, we begin Theraplay Groups with the adults providing safety and nurturing. As trust develops and the children's needs are being met, the children are included in the responsibility of caring for, and keeping each other safe and involved in the games. Blindfold Walk is an excellent example of the leader being responsible for nurturing and safety and beginning to allow the children to take over that responsibility.

The leader says, "OK, everybody stand up and hold hands. Jim, you get to be first. Now I'm going to put this towel over your head so you can't peek. And we have to hold hands and walk Jim all around the room. But we have to watch him and take care of him so he doesn't bump anything. Jim, if we pull you too fast and it gets scary, tell us. OK, Jim, are you ready? What do you want to tell us?"

Jim says, "Don't walk too fast. Don't bump me. And DON'T let go!"

The leader covers Jim up, and guides the class around the room, reminding them all, but especially the children holding Jim's hands, to watch out for him. At the end of Jim's walk, the kids ask, "Did we bump you?" Jim: "No!" Group: "Did we walk too fast?" Jim: "No!" Group: "Were you scared?" Jim: "NO!" The children are all very proud of themselves for taking such good care of Jim, and begin to trust that the others will care for **them** when it is their turn.

Once the children begin to trust each other, they move to the next stage where the underlying issues begin to surface. This is the stage during which interactions between leaders and children, and among the children, can really be used to meet needs and to begin to bring about internally motivated changes in behavior. During this stage, you will provide more stimulating and challenging activities, such as Partner Pull-Ups, Follow the Leader, Touch Blue, Three-Legged Walk, and Funny Faces.

The game for this session is Three-Legged Walk. The leaders pair the children with a piece of yarn loosely tying one leg of one child to the leg of the other. The object is for each pair to make it all the way around the room and back to our circle. Susie, the "Little Adult" is paired with Johnny, who is very impulsive and distractible. Susie starts off in the lead, as usual, expecting that Johnny will follow. But Johnny got distracted by watching another pair, and is not paying attention to Susie. In order to get themselves around the room, Susie finds that she cannot just boss Johnny around—and that she is having fun!—and Johnny has to pay attention to Susie. Because they are having fun, and want to be in the game, they work it out with each other, and finally make it back to loud applause.

The purpose of the Theraplay Group during this stage is to allow problems to arise, and to guide the children's interactions so that they begin finding their own resolutions. You do **not** want to prevent problems or control behavior, but to provide the interactions that will bring about positive change.

Of course, you are going to be very careful that nothing gets out of hand. Safety (emotional and physical) is always the first priority. You will watch the problems carefully, provide guidance, and intervene as needed. During this stage, things can easily get out of control. Expect this and be prepared to deal with it.

In the last stage, it becomes apparent that the children have been internalizing the positive involvement, and are becoming more coopera-tive and nurturing with each other. The group becomes cohesive during this stage, and experiences in the group generalize readily to other situations. It is during this stage that your class will come in from recess and tell you that Johnny fell and bumped his knee, so Freddy gave it a rub. And you notice that during reading class, Johnny knows when it is his turn because he is paying attention; and when he earns a star on his paper, the others congratulate him instead of saying mean things.

As you approach the end of the school year, you will return to activi-ties that are more nurturing and cooperative. Because the group must deal with termination, nurturing activities should be emphasized. The children should also have the opportunity to repeat their favorite games.

This is the time to talk with the children about the group ending, about the fun you have had together, about the ways they have grown ("Remember when Mary always tried to take everyone else's turn? Now she can wait for her own turn.")

An excellent activity for termination is "Special Lists." The leader, using marker and a large piece of blank newsprint, writes, "Johnny's Special List" on top of the page. Then each group member says one special thing he or she likes about Johnny, and the leader writes it down. The lists are put up on a wall, and on the last day of school, each child takes his list home.

If you are just having one Theraplay Group per week, you may want to consider adding an extra session each week to do "Special Lists," and continuing the regular Theraplay Group sessions with playful activities and nurturing games. Plan ahead so that enough time is allowed for each child to have his list made.

Plan at least one activity that produces something concrete for the children to take home as a remembrance of the group and the people in it, for by now, it has surely become a very special experience for them. Writing a group story, drawing pictures and copying them into a packet for each child, taking a group picture and having copies made, are all good ending activities. We mention this here because they also take some planning so that each child has his copy by the last session. Be sure to make one for yourself, also. You will want to have your own remem-brance of your group after it is over.

Chapter 9

THERAPLAY GROUPS FOR
THE SPECIAL EDUCATION TEACHER

Jeanine Tregay

S pecial education teachers are not concerned only with academics. Children are placed in their classrooms because of problems that interfere with their learning and their functioning in a school setting. Because problems of poor self esteem, poor impulse control, inappropriate social interaction and communication difficulties underlie and affect all their behavior, including academic performance, it becomes the teacher's responsibility to find some way to help with those problems so the children will be able to learn. This responsibility is shared with other professionals in the school—social workers, speech therapists, occupational therapists, etc. If the knowledge and the techniques that these professionals bring are coordinated with the teacher's goals, if together all the expertise can be integrated into a total classroom program, the effects of any outside therapies will be increased.

An effective special education classroom cannot exist in isolation, but must become a well-rounded **program** where all facets of support for the children are integrated throughout each day. At its best, all therapy must carry over and become part of the classroom life. To send an individual child for speech, social work, or any type of therapy, for one half hour a week in **isolation** from the rest of the classroom routine is not enough; all therapies become most effective when there is transference into the daily classroom routine. If a child receives speech therapy, for example, then the classroom teacher should be aware of the speech goals so that they can be reinforced throughout the day. If social work is being provided, it should be supported by a focus on social/emotional issues within the classroom. Establishing a Theraplay Group in the classroom, **with the participation of the classroom teacher,** can be a real asset in developing an integrated program which addresses both behavioral and academic needs.

79

Special education teachers, by definition, deal with problems and behaviors that interfere with children's learning. Whether the classification is learning disabilities, educably handicapped, behavior disorders, or communicative disorders, children's social-emotional development is also involved. Often the behaviors that we see can be difficult to manage effectively because it is unclear what they are related to, or what is causing them. A Theraplay Group in a classroom is an extremely effective technique for increasing our understanding of our children and their needs.

Theraplay Groups **allow problems to surface** in order that we can help children manage them in positive growth-enhancing ways. Often the first signs of underlying problems are seen in the Theraplay Group, rather than during classroom instruction or social work sessions, because the group creates a family situation. In fact, these behaviors were probably always present, we just did not understand what they meant. In the Theraplay Group, we gain new insight as to why a child may be behaving in unhealthy ways. Only when we understand his underlying problems can we know how to help the child.

Some examples of how unexpected problems can surface in a Theraplay Group are in order. In my class, Harry seemed to have appropriate social interactions with not only his classmates but the entire school. In social work sessions, he always said the right things. But, in our Theraplay Group, I began to noticed that he did not **act** as he spoke. Harry scooched away from the group, and did not participate as much as I expected. Activities "weren't fun"—he "was bored." When I began to look closer at the way he functioned in other social situations and in the classroom, I realized that he had been covering up his problems very well.

Although Harry got along well with others on a superficial level, he did not develop closer relationships with anyone. He "got bored" easily; he would play a game for a short while and then walk away. He would talk with someone for a few minutes and then leave the interaction. I saw similar behaviors with his schoolwork: many assignments were done quickly but poorly. Although he obligingly worked on every assignment, many were not completed. In effect, he put little effort into either relationships, or into meeting academic expectations. Although at first glance he seemed cooperative and friendly, in actuality he withdrew and isolated himself. By doing so, he created situations in which he was in control, and in which he did not "need" nurturing. He was, in fact, a "Little Adult," and one who was not learning very much.

Not only did Harry's underlying problems emerge most clearly during our Theraplay Group, but that was the time I was most focused on seeing them. Once I had a better understanding of Harry's needs, I was able to find ways to help him.

I knew Joe had problems but had not realized just how bad they were. At first I thought his problems would be relatively simple to modify. It was simply an issue of who was going to control his behavior, of course. If I said, "Take out your pencil," I might get a 20 minute argument about why he wanted to use his marker instead. I did not get very far helping him while I saw him in these terms. Through the Theraplay Group sessions, I began to look at his problems in a different way.

I noticed that Joe's worst behavior occurred when we were using lotion, and I realized that his attempts to always be first, to take everyone else's turn, to focus attention on himself by stopping the game were **not** just attempts to control. He was very **needy**; he needed nurturing; he was afraid he was not going to get it and he did not know **how** to get it. I had been concentrating on providing external structure to control him. It was true that he needed structure, but he also needed nurturing—and that is what I had overlooked. Observing his behavior in the group helped me to see that the issue was not just the standard power struggle. When I concentrated on nurturing Joe **even though he did not "deserve" it and could not show that he wanted it,** his behaviors began to change.

Through the Theraplay Group, children begin to grow because they are experiencing positive relationships. They begin to change their behavior, not because **we** talk at them, but because **they** want to be able to participate in the fun of the group.

The whole class transfers to the rest of the day the supportive and caring atmosphere that develops in the group. And because everyone, including the teacher, has been involved together, these feelings are readily integrated into all the classroom routines.

The children carry over the feelings of trust, safety, and self-confidence they begin to develop in the Theraplay Group.

The teacher carries over the insights gained from observing behavior during Group. As now-familiar issues arise, the teacher applies new ideas and techniques from Theraplay **throughout each day.** The structure of the classroom is affected, and the Theraplay Group becomes an integral part of the over-all program.

Sometimes you will plan to integrate Theraplay techniques into your classroom management. Other times this will begin to happen spontaneously. One day, when I said, "Take out your pencils," Joe took out his marker as usual. I will never forget the look on his face when I started singing, "No, no, no; Joe doesn't want to; no, no, no!" Giving me a look of utter amazement, he took out his pencil!

Let me share an example that illustrates the interplay of a Theraplay Group and other activities in a classroom program. One of the Group activities during the last sessions of the year was "Special Lists." In this activity, each person in the group, including the leader, had a session devoted to his special list. Each group member would say something special about the person which the leader would write down on a large piece of paper. I felt that this was such a successful activity, and meant so much to the children that first year that I decided to expand on it. The next year, in addition to each weekly session with the Theraplay therapist, I scheduled an extra session for "Special Lists." I originally intended this to be a fairly short-term activity. It lasted the entire year and evolved into a productive variation: each of us had to say one thing we liked about the person and one thing we did not like about him. This produced some lively sessions! It was fascinating to me to see how the children were able to zero in on someone else's problem, and equally fascinating to see that they had trouble **recognizing** their **own** problem! This provided our social worker with some very pertinent topics for her discussion group with the class.

The Special List activity continued to affect the program for my class. Toward the end of the school year, I began using behavior contracts with the children. I had tried this technique with previous classes, but it had not been particularly successful. Using behavior contracts in a Theraplay classroom may seem to be a contradiction, but it evolved from our two-part Special List sessions. Since the children were becoming more aware of their actions, I decided to see if we could focus more specifically on the behaviors that had been listed as "likes." The Special Lists sessions turned into contract-writing sessions. This time, instead of hearing what others liked and disliked about him, the child whose turn it was had to choose and talk about his own behavior.

JOE: Well, I think maybe I should cooperate more with my friends.

LEADER: Then what are some things you are going to do to show that?

JOE: I'll let Sam have a turn to be first in line.

LEADER: What are some of the things you can't do if you want to cooperate?

JOE: (thinking hard) I can't grab his cards when we play "Old Maid."

No one was required, or pushed, to have a contract. Several children decided not to have one. Others said that they were not ready to have a contract, so we waited until they decided they were ready. By the end of the year, everyone had a contract.

What is important is that the children had really listened to, and learned from, each other while writing their Special Lists. They were now able to look at some of their problems. I had the sense that they were truly deciding for themselves the behavior they wanted to change. It was no surprise that this time, the contracts were successful!

I discovered that it was the children themselves who initiated much of the carryover of the Theraplay atmosphere. Even though I made an effort to integrate the approach into the daily routine, there were many times when the children were quicker than I was. When a child disrupted a teaching session with misbehavior, my first reaction was to use behavior modification to control it. But it was one of the children who said, "Maybe he needs a lotion rub." Problems became more and more a topic for discussion (rather than time-out or loss of privileges) with much of the advice and suggestions coming from the children. "Jimmy, you should tell him you don't like that." "No hurts." "Why don't you stick together with us?" I discovered that when we took a little time to **deal with** problems, rather than trying to **control** them, the children's attention to lessons actually increased. Most of all, as the children began developing self-control, I was able to spend more time on teaching and less time on "discipline." I was able to increase the amount of mainstreaming into regular classes as the children improved their academic skills and managed their behavior more appropriately.

The children began to cope with their needs, fears, and anger more positively. They became more able to pay attention to academic tasks. They made an effort to learn, and to be less disruptive. Interactions became more appropriate. They began to share, to take turns, to cooperate, and to pay attention to each other. As a result, the whole class began to learn more, began to grow as individuals, and began to get along with each other.

The usual training for special education teachers places more emphasis on ways to control behavior than on ways to be aware of, and to deal with, underlying needs which cause the inappropriate behavior. While it may be necessary to control many behaviors in order to manage a classroom where children can be safe and reasonably productive, this is not enough. It is only the first step. Your real goal is the child's growth in managing his own behavior. If you cannot find ways to help a child to internalize controls, you will have to continue providing external controls. Only if you make changes in what is causing the problem behaviors can you make real progress with the child. If you can focus on meeting children's underlying emotional needs, as well as on behavior management, you will have a far more effective program for your children.

Chapter 10

DIARY OF A THERAPLAY CLASSROOM

We are going to give you a picture of a typical primary behavior disorders classroom, with descriptions of a few of the children, and the kind of progress they made over one- to two-year periods in a program in which the Theraplay philosophy and Theraplay Groups played an integral part.

Joe entered this class at age 7, after 2 years in a early childhood special education program. A chubby, blond, blue-eyed boy, he seemed at first glance to be cheerful and self-confident. With little verbal or physical impulse control, he talked whenever he wanted (most of the time!) about whatever popped into his mind. He seemed always to want to be the center of attention. He was oblivious to other children's rights, or school standards for controls. He displayed little interest in interacting with other children unless he was telling them what to do in a game. He did not share, take turns or cooperate, and demanded to be "number one" in everything.

He engaged in a good deal of surreptitious physical aggression, such as pinching, pushing, shoving in line, or deliberately walking into someone while pretending not to see him. He once deliberately urinated on another child in the bathroom, with no provocation. He **always** had an excuse or reason for why he had either not done what you had just seen him do, or why it was an excusable thing to do—sometimes both! He had the same kind of excuses for doing what he wanted instead of following directions, and was ready to argue interminably about it. His reading level was approximately beginning 1st grade. He sounded out simple words like c-a-t, but did not blend the sounds into "cat." He had the concepts of one digit addition and subtraction, but used his fingers instead of remembering facts.

Sam, whose academic skills were on an equivalent level with Joe's, was 8 years old. He had articulation and language problems; he sounded like a 3 or 4 year old instead of an 8 year old. He frequently asked for help with things like tying shoes or zipping jackets; he **behaved** like a 3 or 4 year old.

He too was very impulsive, with much inappropriate verbalization and wandering around the room. However, he was not physically aggressive; rather, he was isolated and rarely interacted with the other children at all. His idea of play was to choose a simple puzzle and see how fast he could put it together. He sought adult attention and approval constantly, with a veneer of, "Aren't I a wonderful boy?" He became upset when anyone else received positive attention, and had difficulty in attending to any task because he was too busy checking on everyone else. He wanted always to be the best, but was very easily frustrated and frequently dissolved into tears when a task was presented.

Occasionally when very frustrated, he would become self-abusive, putting his fingers down his throat to make himself vomit, literally pulling out clumps of hair from his head, or scratching and biting his arms until they bled. He was nearly always covered with scratches on his face, hands, arms, and legs. He and Joe, who had previously been in the same class, were arch-rivals.

Tim, not quite 7, had also been in the same class as Joe and Sam. He was excessively fearful, withdrawn and confined. He cried frequently for no apparent reason, and was unable to verbalize why he was crying or how he felt. He would continue crying for long periods, until the teacher finally began setting the timer for one minute and telling him he had to stop when it went off. When the buzzer went off, Tim could stop crying and continue his work!

He was excessively concerned that everything run according to schedule, and became upset if there were any changes or if any class period ran late or did not start on time. He flinched from any physical contact—if the class walked down the hall together, he would hug the opposite wall. He seemed fearful of the other children but would occasionally engage in a learning game with another quiet child. During classes, he would answer specific, concrete questions, such as, "What is 2 + 2?" but was otherwise inarticulate, particularly in social interactions. If another child hit him or took his book, he showed no outward reaction, said nothing, but perhaps half an hour later would begin to cry and be unable to explain why.

Interestingly enough, in spite of these problems, he functioned academically at almost his expected grade level in all tasks that were either concrete or depended on memory skills. He had difficulty coping with abstractions (e.g., Is this sentence asking us or telling us?) or tasks requiring inferences or analysis. He was unable to ask for help with his schoolwork.

Dan, age 7, came to school in cowboy boots and a black leather jacket with chains. Swaggering around, he liked to think he was a real tough guy. This illusion was dispelled each day when he unobtrusively held the teacher's hand in the hallway or came up for a hug at the end of a work period. Very unsure of his abilities in school, he had an extremely low frustration tolerance and frequently burst into tears or temper tantrums when he felt he was unable to perform acceptably. In a reading group with one other child, the teacher had to sit holding his hand to help him through it. He had a number of moderate learning disabilities to complicate his life. He had difficulty with frequent reversals in both reading and math, difficulty with sound-symbol association and with remembering math facts. He functioned on a beginning first grade level in most areas. His learning difficulties were exacerbated because he always wanted to rush through tasks as quickly as possible, and did very careless work. He was also very impulsive and distractible.

Georgia, age 6, was a very verbal—and a very disturbed—little girl. She did well academically, but was terrified of making mistakes. Some part of her body was in constant motion: she flapped her hands, wiggled her feet, repeatedly got up and sat down. She talked out loud to herself most of the time, and hummed or sang the rest of the time. She was oblivious to the other children in class, and had virtually no interaction with them. It was almost as if they were objects to her, not other people. She often wet her pants; if she was sent to the bathroom, she forgot to use the toilet. Her speech was always very objective and academic; she did not express her emotions.

Running a weekly Theraplay Group became an integral part of this classroom. Because there was so much carryover into the rest of the classroom, the entire program was strongly influenced by "Group." During the first year of "Group," changes were seen both in individual children and in the class as a whole. This growth continued throughout the second year together. Let us share some of these changes with you.

It is the beginning of the first year together. Four children including Joe and Sam are in a reading group. Sam is looking at the bulletin board on the other wall rather than at the word cards the teacher is displaying. Joe starts talking about what he had for breakfast and while he is talking, he kicks Sam under the table. Later on, they both earn a sticker for reading a group of words correctly. Sam is indignant that Joe got a sticker, while Joe grabs the stickers in order to get first choice. During play time, Sam takes a ten-piece wooden puzzle to his desk and practices how quickly he can put it together. Tim is sitting at the table alone coloring a picture. Joe walks over and breaks one of his crayons. Tim says nothing. About twenty minutes later, when all the children are doing workbook pages at their desks, Tim begins sobbing loudly. He is unable to give any reason for his crying or to respond to questions. Finally, the teacher sets the timer and tells him he has to stop crying in one minute. When the timer goes off, Tim stops crying. The teacher asks again what's the matter, and he replies, "I think I have a headache?" She says, "Sometimes people cry because they feel sad or angry." Tim just looks at her in confusion; he does not know how he feels.

Georgia has been given a writing assignment at her desk. Singing and humming, she walks around her desk, stops to write a word, shakes her hands in the air, walks around her desk again, writes another word. She is truly engrossed in her work, and completely oblivious both of the surroundings and her own actions. During playtime, she wanders around the room singing. When another child is in her way, she knocks him over accidentally as she continues on her way, and does not notice that she has done so, or that the other child is crying. She stops to give the teacher a highly articulate description of a recent trip to New York; she is not really trying to communicate, but is just talking out loud.

Dan is using plastic counters to add 3 and 5. He loses track, decides to write down 6 in order to get the problem done. When the teacher points out that this is a mistake, he throws the counters on the floor, shouts that he hates this school, and rushes crying to his desk. During playtime, he makes a block house, boasting how he can make a real one with a real bulldozer. When someone else reaches for a block he planned to use, he knocks over the other person's building.

The class is having its second or third "Group" session. After remembering the rules, No Hurts, Stick Together, and Have Fun, they are noticing how everyone is today. Georgia keeps taking the leader's turn to notice things about people, so the leader takes Georgia on her lap, saying, "Hey! You keep doing my job! You have to let **me** do my job. This is **my** turn." Georgia is able to relax a little more, within the safe embrace. When it is Sam's turn, the group notices that his hands and arms are covered with scratches. They count 23 scratches! With great glee and a sparkle in his eyes, Sam explains that he held his cat over the toilet so it would scratch him; he **loves** to get hurt, it's the best thing in the world! He has never before been so animated. The teacher says forcefully, "But I don't **like** it when you get hurt! I don't want you to be hurt! The rule is **No Hurts**!! I'm going to put lotion on your hand so I can take care of you." As she gets out the lotion, Joe sticks out his hand with a scratch on it and tries to take Sam's turn, managing to "accidentally" bump Sam while pushing in front of him. The group helps Joe give Sam a gentle rub to make up for it, and to sit back to wait for his turn. The leader makes a chart listing the number of Sam's scratches, and enlists the children to help check next week to see if he has less scratches. Dan puts his hands under his shirt so no one can check him, saying, "Nothing ever hurts me 'cuz I'm tough." The teacher says, "Oh well then, I'll just give you some on your ear!" and she puts lotion on his ear. He then shows the cut on his finger, and she puts lotion around that too. When it is Joe's turn, he puts his hands behind his back and says that he is allergic to lotion. "Well, isn't it lucky that I have some powder for you!" she exclaims, and Joe holds out his hand to have talc patted around his scratch.

A little later in the year, Sam is very frustrated because he cannot do his math. Even though the concept was explained to the class a number of times, he was busy checking on what Joe was doing and did not pay attention. Now he is too frustrated to listen to the teacher's explaining it to him again. He begins whining and crying and saying it is too hard for him. He goes into the corner. Then screaming "I'll never be able to do it!" he clutches at his head and pulls out a clump of hair. The teacher grabs him, shouting "NO! No Hurts! I won't **let** you hurt yourself! You can be mad but you **can't hurt yourself!**"

SOME MONTHS LATER: The group is passing around Funny Faces. Dan passes one to Tim, but Tim misses the face because he is looking down and is withdrawn from the group. Everyone tells him, "Hey, Tim, stick together! We need you to play! Look at Dan so he can pass you the face." Georgia begins to take over, telling Tim what the funny face was like. The leader reminds her that it is Dan's turn. Tim finally gets the funny face from Dan, and is supposed to pass it to the leader, but he does not quite turn to her or make eye contact. She says, "Hey, I didn't get that! Pass it to me so I can have my turn!" When it is Sam's turn to make a funny face, he makes a strange noise instead. The leader says: "Hey! That's a funny noise, not a funny face! You have to play **our** game." He makes another noise. "That's a **noise**. Pass along a funny face!" Sam looks at her blankly: "Like what?" Leader: "Is it my turn? OK, I'll have my turn!" She turns to pass a face to Joe and Sam cries, "I've got one! I'm ready!"

At recess, several of the children are playing a game of Old Maid. Georgia is getting excited and starts to take over; Tim turns to her and says, "Hey! That's **my** turn!"

Georgia has noticed that Danny is making a block building. She sits down next to him and begins making a garage to go with it. After a while, she notices that his building does not match her garage and begins to give him directions. Annoyed, he tells her that he started it first, and continues to do it his own way. She then ignores him and continues her own building, talking to herself about it. Tim and Sam are at the table doing a puzzle together. Tim occasionally points out to Sam where a piece might fit. Joe walks up, takes a puzzle piece out of Tim's hand and begins to work on the puzzle. Tim looks at him but does not say anything.

THAT SPRING: In reading class, both Sam and Joe earn stickers for knowing all the words. Sam looks angrily at Joe and then says to himself, "Oh well, I got a sticker too." Working at his seat, Tim raises his hand to tell me that Dan just bumped his desk. "Well, tell Dan about it." Tim turns red, looks at the floor and mutters "You bumped me and I didn't like it." "Sorry, it was an accident. Want a rub?" and Dan gives Tim a rub on the shoulder.

Joe has been coming to school every morning very angry, aggressive and irritable. He generally manages to cause trouble for everyone and to have a tantrum by 9:30. Finally the teacher says, "All right, Joe. What's going on?" He tells her that every morning he has a fight with his mother about getting ready for school on time, and it makes him feel terrible. The teacher points out that she can understand how he feels, but his behavior is just making things worse; can he think of anything else to do about it? (She has an alternative behavior in mind for him, like getting up earlier to be ready.) He thinks for a minute and then says, "Maybe it would help if you gave me some lotion to make me feel better." Several days later, after getting lotion patted on his cheeks every morning, Joe says to Sam, "Hey Sam, want to play? You can choose the game."

During "Group," they have been counting Sam's "hurts." The last few times, there have been significantly less. Everyone says how glad they are because they do not want people to be hurt, and they all give a cheer for Sam.

THE SECOND YEAR, FALL: When the children come in from

recess, there has obviously been a problem. When the teacher asks about it, Tim stands up, and looking at Joe, says forcefully, "You pushed me down when we were playing and that hurt me! I don't like it! There's not supposed to be any hurts! I don't want to be your friend if you do that." Joe turns red and says, "Aw, I didn't push hard. I was just playing around." "Well you hurt me and I don't like it!" "Sorry," mutters Joe. "Sorry doesn't help," says Dan. "You better give him a rub." Joe looks mutinous. "Come **on**," says Dan, "You have to give him a rub to make up for it." "Joe," explains Georgia, "if you go around hurting people, they won't like you. The only thing to do is make up for it and try not to do it again." Joe gives Tim a rub on the back.

THAT WINTER: It has been some time since Sam has had more hurts than could be expected of any eight year old boy. During a Group session, the leader discovers a big angry scratch on the back of his neck, and asks what happened. He tells her that his older sister did it when she was fighting with him. "Sam, I want you to give your sister a message from me. Tell her I said that I don't like it when you get hurt. Tell her I said I don't want there to be any hurts." A few weeks later, Sam comes up to her. "Teacher, do you remember that message you sent to my sister about no hurts? Could you please send it to her again?" This from the boy who once said being hurt was the best thing in the world!

THAT SPRING: The teacher is out on the playground on recess duty when Dan and Tim come up to her, escorting a defiant and frightened-looking child from one of the first grade classes. Dan: "Teacher! We were playing and this kid hit Tim on the arm!" Tim (encouraged by Dan's support): "Yeah! and I didn't like it." The teacher asks the first-grader what he has to say and he mutters that he didn't really mean it, and he's sorry. Dan tells the first grader, kindly, "That's not enough. You have to make him feel better. Give him a rub on his arm." The first grader looks at Tim and tentatively pats his arm. Tim says gruffly, "OK, but remember, no hurts." And the three of them go off to play.

It has become automatic in the classroom for the children to give each other a rub or a pat when they have done something to hurt another child. This comes naturally to them, showing their greater awareness that the other child is a real person like themselves. There are increasing instances of the children playing and working together cooperatively, and trying to understand and help with each other's problems. Not that the old problems have disappeared. But there are many more positive behaviors occurring, both socially and academically.

At the end of two years with these children, the teacher assesses their progress.

Tim, the boy who was so frightened and withdrawn and confused, is mainstreamed at grade level for three classes, and recently had to be scolded for hitting someone! He now expresses his feelings, and asserts himself when he needs to.

Georgia, the girl who could not sit still at all and walked through other children as though they did not exist, is able to work seated at her desk for half hour periods—sometimes even longer—and to actually play together for short periods with other children. She sang in the school chorus and joined Brownies.

Sam, the boy who loved being hurt and could not attend to learning tasks, is now seeking protection. In both math and reading he has improved nearly three years in a two year period—a child whose behavior problems interfered with his learning!

Joe too has improved in both math and reading 2.5 years in two years. This impulsive, aggressive attention seeker can now sit at his desk and work independently at an assigned task. He is, at least some of the time, seeking more appropriate ways of dealing with his anger.

The "famous tough guy," Dan, still wears his leather jackets and cowboy boots, but he has become the real care-taker in the group, always sensitive to another child's hurt and getting the class to "stick together." Because of learning disabilities, his academic progress has been less than that of the others. However, he has learned to read and to do beginning math. More important, he works carefully now and has learned to ask for help when he becomes frustrated instead of having a tantrum.

Something is working.

For three years, the teacher tracked the changes in each child's test scores. Every child gained at least one year's grade level, in both reading and math, per academic year. This was a much greater rate of progress than any of them had shown previously, even those who had been in other special education classes. When you consider that these are children whose behavioral problems interfered substantially with their learning, this is remarkable progress. Similarly, each child made progress achieving more school-appropriate behavior. The real significance of the improved behavior is that it came about, not through acceptance of the controls externally imposed on the classroom (though these were certainly used initially), but rather through the internalization of controls. The teacher measured this internal growth through observing the increase in spontaneously exhibited behavior that reflected Group goals: cooperation, taking turns, sharing, asserting, attending to others, etc., with the criteria that these behaviors occurred in relatively unstructured, not directly supervised, settings (school hallways, recess, lunch, etc.).

Although the increase in more appropriate social behavior could certainly be seen during Group sessions, the **real** test was seeing these behaviors during other times in the classroom and in school. The teacher overheard children telling each other at recess, "Don't be so rough! No hurts!" It was one of the **children** who began the extension of the Group practice of giving a gentle rub when you had hurt someone, and soon the whole class had, on their own, adopted this as standard practice. It was one of the **children** who began asking for a lotion rub to help make him feel better when things went wrong. Again, the rest of the children adopted this.

There was no research study made of the effects of using Theraplay Group techniques in this classroom. However, we, as well as the teacher, were convinced that the behavioral and academic progress described was indeed related to these techniques.

The longer a Theraplay Group is used in a classroom, the more its effects will expand. You will find that you no longer have a class with a Theraplay Group, but that you now have "A Theraplay Classroom."

Chapter 11

THERAPLAY GROUPS FOR
THE PRIMARY CLASSROOM TEACHER

Mary Alice Dacosse[1]

Learning to lead Theraplay Groups sounded ideal to me. Fitting it into my schedule created a problem, but somehow I suspected it would be worth the effort. Having taught both special education and second grade, I was finding kindergarten a little more challenging than I had anticipated. The same problems that had existed in my other classrooms were present at the kindergarten level as well. School should have **some** fun, but the daily problems confronting us frequently made fun impossible. With its nurturing, structuring activities that emphasized feeling good and having fun, a Theraplay Group had great appeal.

My students were suffering from the signs of the times. Many came from divorced or single parent families. Many were "latch-key kids" who had the TV for a baby sitter or older brothers or sisters as guardians. Many were being raised by grandparents. Some came from "low economic, culturally deprived" environments. Most of them were unhappy. They needed a mother, they needed a nurse, they needed a friend. They needed support, they needed security, they needed self-confidence. They needed to know they were special, and special for who they were. I needed help, help, and more help. What we ALL needed was a Theraplay Group.

But my classroom was not unique. A "problem" or "needy" child is found in any class. These children are not confined to a certain population, geographic area, or economic status. There is at least one child (don't we wish it was only one?) who screams to you for attention. Worse yet, there are those who silently yell his or her needs to you. These children will sound familiar to you: the child who is a slow reader and shies away from the group; the chronic complainer; the impulsive child who turns in his work first and the one who always turns in his work last; the giggler, the pincher, the name caller, the squirmer; the child who never raises his hand—and the one who ALWAYS raises his hand!

I do not promise that a Theraplay Group will solve all of these problems or make them magically disappear. But a Theraplay Group **will** make a difference. It not only addresses these problems, but also provides a support system for the teacher.

As teachers, we have problems arising from outside sources as well as from within the classroom. There is increased pressure from society for us to raise test scores, broaden the curriculum, and prove teacher accountability. We are constantly under pressure to produce. Thus, we use all the teaching tools at our disposal to motivate our children. Even in kindergarten, the children soon regard us as the ones who can make or break them with a smiley face stamp, a star next to their name, or a pizza scented smelly sticker. These demands have placed a heavy emphasis on the teacher's role as "The Grader." Teachers are, of course, more than this.

Theraplay Groups will give you the opportunity to sit with your class and give warm, caring, nurturing attention. Thus, Theraplay Groups enable you to be more than "just a teacher," simply by BEING more with your students. Of course you are with your students all day long as it is. But it is not as easy to really BE WITH them when you are constantly judging them. And they know it! This puts pressure on the child to please, to act out in rebellion, or to simply give up trying. In Theraplay Groups, the children do not have to worry about pleasing or performing. Theraplay is a different experience for them. They get to be who they are, and to be appreciated for that, not just for what they can do. And they get to have fun.

Fun became the primary focus of my Theraplay Groups. Let me explain why.

The elements of Theraplay can be seen as forming a flexible hierarchy. Nurturing comes first. This is the foundation upon which Stimulation, Structure, and Challenge rest. A child who has had little, or not enough, nurturing will need a primary focus on that type of interaction in his relationships. While there has been a clear emphasis on nurturing in most of the other chapters in this book, this chapter is different. Why? Because I found that most of my kindergarten children were able to go beyond that level. Obviously they had had "good-enough" nurturing because their need for it (and we always need it) was easily met with lotion, Baby Wipes, and eventually with just blowing kisses. Once my role as a nurturer was established, they knew where they could get it. They felt secure. They were ready, **and therefore needed,** to move up the hierarchy to stimulating and challenging activities.[2] They needed an emphasis on FUN.

It is important to have fun in the school environment where there are not many opportunities for fun besides recess, music, and gym. Children, and adults as well, benefit from fun that is incorporated into their classroom routine. Theraplay brought this quality into our classroom, a classroom that had the responsibility to address the young child. A young child who too soon becomes goal-oriented, grade-oriented, task-oriented, may lose sight of the importance of fun in his life. So HAVING FUN became our primary focus.

However, I now became concerned about bringing "too much fun" into the classroom. How do you have fun with a large group and not lose control? Perhaps this sounds familiar: "Class, if you keep this up, we won't be able to have fun again. (No change except that the class now becomes louder to drown out your voice!) Alright, that's it! You blew it now. We can't have any more fun!" Whatever the activity, it probably was not much fun anyway! But you do not have to sacrifice control in order to have fun. A Theraplay Group enables you to maintain structure in a large group without stifling enjoyment.

Your students come to recognize this. They understand that you are doing the structuring so that the group can be successful. They appreciate it because they experience the safety and security that your structuring brings. It also brings them attention they may otherwise not have received, fixes their hurts, does not pressure them to perform, and lets them have fun! And you become a symbol for these feelings because this Group has come from you.

Theraplay Groups are easy to structure with just three basic rules: NO HURTS! STICK TOGETHER! HAVE FUN! And the children love the rules! These rules are easy to remember, make a lot of sense and preserve that precious commodity: **fun.** The rules put a stop to anyone tempted to pinch, squeeze, kick or bring forth the cry, "Teacher, she's bothering me!" You now have an entire class of children who are striving to preserve peace, and they will be more than willing to remind someone of these rules. Nicely of course!

At this point, you may think it difficult for one adult to lead a large Theraplay-style group. If you wish additional support, you might arrange for a teacher's aide to come at Group time. You may have a student teacher, or your school may encourage older students to help out in the younger grades for part of the day. I did not have a teacher's aide until my third year of leading a Theraplay Group. (She probably benefited even more from participating in the group than I benefited from having her.) As she learned about the children, we developed a shared basis for discovering their needs. She was then able to carry over what she learned from Group into the rest of the classroom activities. This was ideal for both of us.

However, while having an aide may be a bonus, it is not a necessity. In the typical primary classroom, one teacher can lead a group alone. I did. My colleague teaching first grade did. The children **themselves** become your helpers in promoting the Theraplay atmosphere.

Now that your burden of being the disciplinarian has been lightened and you have your Theraplay Group under control, you can relax and experience success as well. Soon you will realize that you are getting through to children you previously could not reach. You watch solemn faces begin to brighten up with smiles. You find out that Carl has a great sense of humor, shy little Susie shines in a group, and that Laura has a delightful little laugh. You get the rare opportunity to be with your students and to enjoy them. What's more, you do not have to plan far in advance, reserve any equipment or sign up for the auditorium. Weekly notes do not have to go home asking parents to send bottle caps or margarine tubs to school. It takes relatively little effort for this wonderful experience to occur.

A Theraplay Group teaches the children (and you too) that even in a large group, they can experience intimacy and pleasure in a safe, cooperative atmosphere. And it feels good! Not only have you established a good feeling throughout the group, but in each individual as well. Each child develops a sense of, "Hey, I LIKE this!" The children have fun, and their self-esteem soars. They have experienced success, whether on their own, with a friend or partner, or as part of the whole group.

Let me share with you how I brought Theraplay Groups into my classroom, introduce you to some of my students, and describe how they benefited from these Groups.

First, we established the rules. Number one was "Stick Together." We sat in a circle, with our legs crossed and everybody's knees touching (and I mean knees touching so as not to break the "charm" of the circle). When we were reciting the rules, one child called out, "Sticked together like glue," and that "stuck" with us for the rest of the year. We stuck together like glue and formed a large, yet intimate and cohesive group.

Rule number two was "No Hurts." I told them we would "fix" all hurts because it was hard to enjoy ourselves if anyone had a hurt. (And even too much noise or loud voices can "hurt" our ears.) In the beginning, EVERYONE had hurts! Most were invisible. Some children had real scars (and a story to go with them), while others searched for anything that could resemble a "hurt." No matter. We took care of them all with lotion. Some days we did not do much else. I thought I would have to buy stock in Johnson and Johnson! But as long as the children NEEDED to have a hurt, we needed to fix them. As the year went on, and the hurts lessened, we were able to fix hurts just by blowing kisses.

The third rule was the most important: "Have Fun!" I tried to give my best "I mean business" look, and told the class that we **had** to have fun. Of course, while you are learning, there may be days when it will not feel quite like fun. I remember when I was new at it, feeling that it was more like **work** than fun. But eventually, that changed. Be patient. The idea and feeling of fun will come to you, too.

We called our Theraplay Group "The Sunshine Group" because we opened the session with the song, "You Are My Sunshine." Almost all of the activities I used were centered on the children's faces and bodies. One-to-one eye contact, so difficult to achieve with children who are not sure of themselves, proved not difficult at all when we played a game focusing on their beautiful eyes, soft noses, or ticklish chins.

My first try at leading a Theraplay Group was with my morning kindergarten class. We sang our song, passed around Eskimo kisses, and fixed hurts. It felt pretty good. Eddie and Tracey did not smile or really participate, but then they never did in other activities, so it was no surprise to me that this was not any different.

My afternoon class was really excited about Group. They loved anything that took them away from "work." Carl was in this class. When Carl had first come to school, his mother had informed me that he had a few problems. One was that, if he did not get his way, he ran around the room, screaming at the top of his lungs and would bang his head against the wall if he was not stopped. I quickly learned to get to Carl before the wall did!

I tried to keep to my schedule and have Group at a designated time and day. However, one day Carl had his typical tantrum. (His typical reason: "Somebody looked at me funny.") I soon had hold of him and was sitting in a chair, quietly rocking him until he could calm down. Carl loved this, but then the rest of the class "looked at ME kind of funny." Then I had an idea! I called for "Sunshine Group" right then and there. I knew Carl loved "Sunshine Group" and the rest of the class was delighted with this spur-of-the-moment idea. Though not in my lesson plan, it was just what we needed. The children gathered around Carl and me, and we had Group. These spontaneous groups were the most meaningful because they came at the time when we most needed them. Sometimes we sat and sang to Carl while I held him. Other times Carl would voluntarily sit next to me and participate in the group. This enabled Carl to come back and be part of the class. Theraplay Group was working!

I was not the only one to recognize the benefits of our Theraplay Group. One day in Group we sang our song, said our rules, fixed our hurts with Baby Wipes, and looked into each other's eyes with a magnifying glass. We were playing "Detective" and some children really scrutinized their partner's face, ears, mouth, etc., while others just focused on one eye. Soon everyone was laughing at the magnified features. Even Eddie! Before I realized it, the other children called out, "Look, Eddie is laughing!" I did not know that the children had been aware of Eddie's non-smiling face. I had never pointed it out because I did not want to add pressure by calling attention to him. The Theraplay Group allowed Eddie to smile when HE was ready. Soon, Eddie was smiling more during other classroom activities as well.

Jimmy was a good boy. He always wanted to help the teacher. He would go where the children were playing but he would not play WITH them. In Sunshine Group, he would not go so far as to refuse to participate, but he would not really join in either.

One day, around Easter time, we played Magical Colors. In this game, an empty egg carton and a dry paint brush is passed around and each child "paints" his neighbor's face. Of course, magical colors are invisible. But not to Jimmy! He held the egg carton for his artist and called out the colors he wanted to be used on his face. He knew just what the colors were and where they were in the carton. (He was so confident I even took a peek to see where "orange" was!) Jimmy sat very still, pointing to the "paint" while his artist "painted." And did he paint!

Jimmy's artist had to push Jimmy's nose up so he could "see" to paint a mustache, then gently folded back Jimmy's ears so he could get to the back of them, almost elbowing Jimmy's eye in the process! But Jimmy never complained. Yet at any other times this much closeness and physical contact would have made Jimmy very uncomfortable. But now he beamed! The rest of the group congratulated the boys on the "work of art." Jimmy, holding his head erect so as not to disturb the masterpiece, went on to return the favor and paint his friend with equal enthusiasm.

Tracey was very shy. She came to school and did her work very diligently but would not talk or play with the other children. She preferred to be on her own, sitting and reading a book. When we had Sunshine Group, she would sit with us with her finger in her mouth and just watch. I told her I was so glad she was there because she helped to round out the circle. Neither I nor the other children ever mentioned her lack of participation. Sometimes I would try to cajole her into the fun but I never pushed her.

After several weeks of Theraplay Group, we were playing "Make a Round Circle." This game was an old DaCosse family favorite. It is a guessing game that requires one child to sit with his back to the group while I trace a circle on his back. Then, the whole group chants, "Make a round circle, color it purple, S.O.M.E.B.O.D.Y. poke!" Then I point to someone to come and gently poke the center of the "circle." The child who has been "poked" must guess the one who did the poking! After we played a while, I pointed to Tracey. Without any hesitation she came and "poked." Then it was her turn. After she guessed twice, her turn was over. She started to get up, but stopped and quietly asked if she could have another turn. I was delighted. When I looked to the rest of the children, there was a silent pause and then they all started to clap! We were more than happy to give Tracey her extra turn. From then on, Tracey joined in a little more each time.

Such moments demonstrate what a wonderfully effective tool Theraplay Groups are in the classroom. It is exciting to watch group cohesiveness develop as the children become concerned for each other and take it upon themselves to get the lotion and fix a hurt. You will be amazed to hear and see children blossom in your class. But it does not end here. Your Theraplay Group is an on-going process. Not only does it create an atmosphere that permeates your classroom, but next year's class will come to you with stories from their siblings and friends about your Sunshine Group. And soon, another group of children will be growing under the nurturing care of your Theraplay Group.

ENDNOTES

1. Mary Alice DaCosse received a B.A. from St. Mary's College, Notre Dame, IN. She has a background in both elementary education and special education, and currently teaches kindergarten in District 89, Maywood, IL. She was one of the first eight Theraplay Group trainees.

2. If the adult does not respond to the child's cues that he is ready to move to the next level, the child's growth will be restricted. If you were to stay at nurturing, for example, when the child's predominant need was for stimulation, you would be actively **holding him back.**

Chapter 12

METAMORPHOSIS: THE TEACHER AS LEADER

Jeanine Tregay

When it was first suggested that I should consider learning how to lead my own classroom Theraplay Group, my reaction was instantaneous: NO WAY! I immediately had a long list of excellent reasons why it could not possibly work and why it would not be a good idea to even try.

A year and a half later, reluctantly and with many misgivings, I decided to try. The year and a half of Rubin's' encouragement and support helped, but to be honest, what really decided it was the threat that, because of cutbacks, we might not **have** a group if I did not lead it.

After leading my group for two years, I could no longer imagine being able to teach a classroom without leading a Theraplay Group.

There are distinct advantages—and disadvantages—in the classroom teacher acting as Theraplay Group leader. In many ways, this presents a unique situation, quite different from having another professional come into the room to act as leader.

I think the issues that I struggled with for that one and a half years are extremely valid, and need to be carefully considered by **anyone** who considers leading a Theraplay Group and particularly by any teacher thinking of leading her own group.

There were four main issues I had to resolve: (1) the feeling of incompetence, that even with training I might fail at what I saw as a very different task than I was used to; (2) a reluctance to add an extra burden that I knew would take a great deal of concentration and energy when I already had more than enough to do; (3) a fear that my role as group leader would conflict with my role as teacher, undermining my authority as teacher and structurer; (4) a feeling that part of what made the Theraplay Group special was that it was led by an "outsider" who came in at a special time, someone who was not around all the time and was not connected with all the day-to-day problems and happenings in the classroom.

What I learned through my experience is that these are difficult issues, but that there **are** ways of dealing with them, and that the benefits that come from the teacher acting as leader outweigh the difficulties.

When I began acting as a leader, I was fortunate to have support and training from a Theraplay therapist. She occasionally acted as co-leader in my session. I videotaped all sessions and we met weekly to analyze them.

I found that in the beginning, I not only felt incompetent, I **was** incompetent! The interesting thing was that the **children** did not know that! And I had to remind myself, as I reminded them about their schoolwork, that I could not expect to know it all right away. The initial sessions were very difficult for me; I was very tense about "doing it right" and making sure it was a **good** session. It was hard to give up being the teacher, being the authority figure, being in control of the children's behavior as differentiated from being in **charge** of keeping the group secure. This is a difference critical to a Theraplay Group and one that takes time to develop.

It was the day when I finally said to myself, "Oh, what the heck! I'm tired of trying to do it right. I'm going to just relax and have fun." And then it finally began to work! That was the session where I **felt** what it was like to be the Group leader, and **felt** how the sessions would begin to take shape. That was the first of many sessions where I too had fun. And maybe that is the real secret of it all: that the children see themselves, reflected in the leader's eyes, as people who are special enough to have fun with. When I stopped worrying about it, I started to become more competent.

I cannot deny that acting as a Theraplay Group leader is an added burden. However, I always felt energized **during** sessions; it was when they were over that I felt drained. (This was **my** reaction. This does not happen to everyone leading a group.) So I always scheduled my sessions at the end of the day so that the children would leave almost immediately.[1] Then I had time to recuperate and think about how the session had gone. The added burden also paid off in time by making other tasks less difficult. There was improvement in the behavior of individual children as some of their needs were met in "Group" sessions so that less time was needed for managing disruptions. As the class gradually took more responsibility for their own behavior, I was able to put more energy into building self-esteem and encouraging positive behaviors. Along with the children, I felt more relaxed and nurtured in the "Theraplay Atmosphere."

Before I began leading my Theraplay Group, I thought there would be a conflict between my role as group leader and my role as teacher. I had thought that as a teacher, I had to be an authority figure, and impose structure. I worried that when I sat down as a Theraplay leader, and responded to the children's needs in a way that was not "controlling," it would cancel out my effectiveness as a teacher/structurer. I also thought that it would confuse the children to have me taking two roles that I saw as being very different. These are common concerns of teachers. Let me reassure you: once I resolved this conflict, I realized it had never really existed except in my own mind. But it was only in going through the experience that I learned this.

I found that, as the group leader, I was still the structurer, but one with a different approach to structuring. I came to appreciate that structuring is not just giving instructions and setting limits. It is not just saying, "You're not earning your points because you didn't do 'x'." It is finding another way of getting **the child** to want to do it. The Theraplay techniques that I learned influenced my teaching style and actually enhanced my role as a teacher. Theraplay techniques gave me extra tools to use as a teacher. Yet I never had any hesitation in imposing firm controls and rules when necessary, and I think the children were more cooperative with my controls because they felt more included than acted upon.

Each year that I acted as Theraplay Group leader, I felt more comfortable and more competent both as Group leader and as a special education teacher. And each year I became more convinced of the benefits of this technique.

To the issue of having a "real" Theraplay therapist lead the group, I had the following thoughts. When an "outsider" comes in to run a Theraplay Group, she does not have an already established, on-going relationship with the group members. She is not dealing with left-over feelings and unfinished business from the rest of the day or week or year! She is not already angry and frustrated—or at least not with THIS group. So in a sense, she is starting "fresh." I thought it would be a little easier for another person to make this time seem more special (and thus more motivating) to the children. Certainly it would be easier for this outsider to be more accepting of the children. I thought this was what made the Theraplay Group work, and that if I led it, daily tensions would make it difficult to have fun. One theory struck down!

This very situation is a real advantage for the classroom teacher, whose role more nearly approximates a parental role than does that of any other professional. The knowledge of the children and the relationships established among us, sometimes over 2 or 3 years of being together all day, can give the teacher a real head-start in planning goals and activities for the group sessions.

There were often some difficult situations, however, that arose while I was leading these groups. If a child and I had had an angry confrontation earlier in the day, I needed to make some decisions: Could these feelings (both mine and the child's) be set aside, be **finished**, because the episode was over and now we were moving on? If feelings of anger, frustration, disappointment, etc., were still hanging on, could this be dealt with in the Group session? It might be quite obvious that the child was really unable to participate in a group session, and I would have to deal with this, both for the child and the rest of the group, before the session began. Sometimes I felt unable to participate in a group at that time and I said so, while providing an alternate occupation for the class. In fact, when I chose to handle my feelings this way, the children were relieved that they were not required to "put their feelings away" just so we could have Group as scheduled. Of course, we would discuss the problem and reschedule as soon as possible.

This flexibility for scheduling is one of the great advantages the classroom teacher has. We can schedule Group for the time that is best for us and our class. The social worker or Theraplay therapist may only be able to come on Tuesday at 3:00, so you have Group then or do without. When the teacher is the leader, she can reschedule for 9:30 on Wednesday and if that does not work out, there is still the rest of the week. You can even spontaneously have a Group when conditions seem right for it, picking up on something that is already happening in the class.

I decided, eventually, that it was actually more beneficial to have the group led by the teacher rather than by an outside therapist; that the things I had seen as disadvantages were actually advantages. I could structure the Group sessions to pick up on issues that had come up during the day, whereas an outside therapist would not know about them. An "outsider" might not know the difference between a child's acting out a real problem and just being "silly," but I did. I think that having the Group led by the teacher was a strong force in its integration into classroom life that could never have happened as effectively with any "outsider."

Theraplay Groups meant a lot to the children in my classroom. I found that when the groups were led by an outside therapist, the children looked forward to the sessions and would ask when we were going to have them. When **I** began to lead the groups myself, the children **always** knew when it was time for Group, and often requested extra sessions. When they were promoted into the next class, they would come to tell me that they missed Group.

I went back to visit my old class one December after I had left my school district. When I walked in the room, the most severely disturbed child in the class looked up and saw me; his face lit up and he cried, "Oh, Mrs. Tregay! Now we can have Group!"

The entire Theraplay Group experience intensified **for all of us** when I was the leader. Having sole responsibility for the Group meant that I had to be even more deeply involved in it; and it made more of an impact on me! Also, I think that when an "outside person" came in to lead Group, the whole experience was seen by all of us—myself included —as something set a little apart, a special event given to us by someone else. But when we were the only ones involved, it was even more important to us. It was **ours** and it was **always with us** throughout the day.

In terms of myself, I felt that I made a lot of personal and professional growth when I learned to act as Theraplay Group leader. Professionally, it expanded my understanding of the children's needs and behaviors, and gave me new techniques for guiding the class. Personally, I had to overcome my reluctance to try something new, something that I sensed would change **me** to a certain extent. I had to put energy into learning something that would change things when I was already comfortable with the way things were. I was proud of myself, and still am, for making the effort that is involved in any growth.

I think every teacher should be **aware** of the principles of Theraplay; this is important knowledge. I do not think, however, that using these techniques will fit in with every teaching style and viewpoint, or be appropriate for all classes. But if you are thinking: "That really sounds like fun!" or "I wonder if maybe that would help some of the children in my class." or "Gee, that sounds like some of the things I already do with my class", then I would encourage you to learn more about leading Theraplay Groups. It may be a struggle, but it is well worth it.

ENDNOTE

1. Other teachers have felt differently, scheduling their groups first thing in the morning as a way to greet children and set the tone for the day. Choice of when to schedule is always an individual preference.

Chapter 13

THERAPLAY GROUPS FOR
THE SOCIAL WORKER/COUNSELOR

We write this chapter with a great appreciation for the contribution Theraplay Groups can give to social work and for what the field of social work has given to Theraplay Groups. Both authors have worked with social workers while at PAEC, and these contacts have shaped and enriched our thinking about the importance and usefulness of Theraplay Groups in education. Many of the ideas we present here emanated from our collaboration with Diane Mirabito, ACSW, who was a social worker at PAEC. She first learned about Theraplay while co-leading individual Theraplay sessions with Rubin, then co-leading a year-long classroom Theraplay Group again with Rubin, and subsequently leading her own social work classroom Theraplay Group.

Theraplay Groups offer social workers a valuable technique for increasing their ability to help children in groups. Social workers often are expected to service a wide range of children with extremely varying needs. A school counselor or social worker may work with children ranging in ages from five to eighteen. In special education, children can range in age from 0 to 21 years! They may be mildly to profoundly affected by their disability, and can have retardation, speech/language problems, autism, motor-, physical-, vision-, and/or learning-disabilities. Without any of the those disabilities, children can have behavior or emotional problems. Certainly, one group approach does not fit all!

Groups often use verbal discussion, peer influence, and self-direction to affect growth and change. But Theraplay Groups have an added dimension.

Based on parent/child interactions, the Theraplay Group approach offers social workers and counselors a highly effective method to use with young children, children who are "young" developmentally, children of any age who have a need for nurturing, and children with language problems who may have trouble with a more verbal group. We have found that using Theraplay is an inviting way of **starting** a group. Let us look at groups from a Theraplay perspective.

PARENT/INFANT INTERACTIONS

We know that parent/infant interactions **start with the parent and go toward the child.** Here is what the parent/infant interaction looks like:

1. Parents do not wait for their child to start a positive interaction. As adults who instinctively know what is best for their baby, **they** make the overtures.

2. At first, parents initiate interactions without expecting the child to return the "healthy interaction." Only after the baby starts to gaze or smile do the parents have the hope of receiving something back from their baby. With troubled children, we must go back to **initiating without expectations,** or the child may never receive the interactions he needs.

3. Parents initiate healthy interactions regardless of whether their baby is "good" or not. Parents do not use "time out." A baby does not have to "be good" in order to be treated "good" by his mother or father.

4. Parents **non-verbally demonstrate** their love for, and commitment to, their baby, they do not only talk about it. A mother of a new-born does not simply say to her baby, "I love you," and let the baby lie there isolated. She constantly demonstrates this love in a way the baby can **feel:** by responding when he cries; by caring for him, feeding him, gazing into his eyes as she sings to him; by smiling with delight when he gurgles, etc.

RECREATING PARENT/INFANT INTERACTIONS IN THE THERAPLAY GROUP

With their foundation in parent/infant interactions, Theraplay Groups have unique characteristics.

1. The leader of the group takes an active/directive role.
2. The group is experience-oriented rather than discussion-oriented.
3. The group has a highly nurturing emphasis.
4. The leader uses unique methods of positive structuring.
5. The group is playful and spontaneous.

The Leader Takes an Active/Directive Role

As an active-directive leader, YOU first will be the nurturer. YOU must feel and show acceptance of each child, and YOU will show pleasure in what he **does** (not necessarily in what he accomplishes or in how conforming he is). Only after receiving these interactions from **an adult** will the child begin to act more appropriately. This is what we mean when we say that in Theraplay Groups, change occurs through experience. The child **experiences** our enjoyment of him, our confidence, our insistence on nurturing him despite his age, our continuing to challenge him despite his excuses and complaining. We have a positive and healthy view of him, and we refuse to let him talk us out of it. Thus will he slowly incorporate **our view** into **his view** of himself. Because we nurture him, he will begin to nurture others. Because we are pleased to be with him, he will later be able to feel pleasure when he is with others. Because we demonstrate concern, he will begin to care for himself. Because we encourage him despite his fears, he will begin to tackle new situations on his own. We convey these messages via the Theraplay atmosphere as we move through the Theraplay session and beyond.

Active/directive leadership relates also to how you lead the session. We already know that Theraplay is the antithesis of play therapy, in which children are allowed to choose what they will play with and how they will play with it. Play therapy provides an important environment for those troubled children who cannot handle closeness and therefore need some space and freedom. But a Theraplay Group says, "I know that you have needs, I know what you need, I know you cannot wait, and I know you need to know that I recognize and can fulfill your needs. And I will do it NOW."

Thus, your Theraplay Group will be directed by YOU. YOU will decide on the activities, who will do what, when, how, where, etc. There may be sessions during which you decide to give the children some choices, but the important thing is that **you** decide it. This does not mean that you do not take into account what the children are communicating. You can use their messages to decide to do a different activity, etc. Because you are empathic, accepting, and responsive to them at all times, your decisions will always reflect their needs. That is the ideal. That is what you are striving to achieve. To relate this to the roots of Theraplay, that is what mothers do: they are in charge of constantly responding to the child. Not giving in to demands, but responding to basic needs. There is a big difference.

The Group is Experience-Oriented

When Diane Mirabito was working with Rubin, co-leading Theraplay sessions, the fact that Theraplay is experience-oriented immediately struck her as different from her instincts and her training. This awareness happened during the following session.

They were working with an expertly manipulative boy, Tommy, who happened to be taller than either one of them. He was constantly attempting to leave the scene, and they were always pulling him back to the mat. Rubin decided to challenge him to a game of staying on the mat. She found a black spot on the mat and told Tommy that it was HIS SPOT and that he had to sit right on top of it. Then, each time he wiggled off, she immediately said, "Oops, you're off the spot! Hurry and get back on." "Oh, oh! I can see your spot! Better cover it up again!" With this game, they no longer had to physically grab him (that is not fun). They found a way to structure him positively and playfully. They also did not try to discuss with Tommy why he kept wanting to run away. Where would that have gotten them? If they had been honest with themselves, they already knew why he wanted to run away: to be in control; to disrupt their plans; to make them mad at him; to get them to verify that he was "bad." But they had a philosophy, and the techniques to back it up, that allowed them to provide playful structure without communicating that Tommy was "bad" when he left the structure. Consequently, they were able to interact in positive games together.

At the end of this session, Mirabito told Rubin that as the session progressed she had had the impulse to discuss with Tommy why he kept getting off his spot. She said, "Now I understand something about Theraplay. You didn't talk about why he got off his spot. You just made a game out of his sitting on the spot. I kept wanting to talk to him, but I realized that wasn't what you were doing. Making a game out of structuring really worked!"

This description of a session clearly demonstrates the action-orientation of Theraplay. However, as with most Theraplay examples there is some overlap, and it also speaks to Theraplay's active/directive style of leadership, and its unique techniques for positive structuring. We felt, however, that it showed dramatically how Theraplay would deal with a problem in terms of actions, rather than by discussion.

As a Theraplay Group leader, when a child continuously does something inappropriate, disruptive, or unhealthy, you will not ask him why he did it. You will take direct action to make a clear and forceful impact on the problem. (More overlap: When you do this, you are taking an active role as leader.) It may be that you hold a child's hand through the remainder of the session. Or, if someone gets hurt, that you immediately react with animated concern, checking the hurt and helping (not asking if he wants to make amends) the hurter to lotion around the hurt. You initiate ACTIONS that are constructive, supportive, and healthy, between members of the group.

Why do we not discuss what happened and talk about more appropriate behavior? What is the reason for focusing on actions?

So often we easily fall into telling children what to do, or how we feel, without **demonstrating** how we feel in very concrete, basic ways. For children, talking about their behavior or how much you care about them, is not enough. Children learn by **doing** — our **doing** as well as their **doing.**

Let us first look at it from the standpoint of what we DO. Instinctively, you know that children "listen" to what we **do**, rather than to what we **say.** You are probably working with children right now who have parents who can say all the right words but whose actions do not fit those words. As their children fight, these parents say, "Johnny, come sit by me so you won't get hurt," and then ignore the fact that their children continue to fight. They are **saying** they care about their children and are concerned that they do not get hurt, yet their actions do not show this.

If you have worked with older children or adults who were able to understand that you cared for them by the verbal communication you gave, this could occur only because, as children—even infants—they experienced parental actions that meshed with the caring words their parents spoke. The troubled children we work with often have not had concrete demonstrations of nurturing, stimulation, structure, and challenge. They need these demonstrations to benefit from help given in discussion format. Providing these messages in the demonstrative, action-oriented way typical of Theraplay will be a clear, direct way of building trust in your group, and will go straight to the heart of the child's primitive needs for healthy parenting/interactions.

Now let us look at **doing** from the child's side. Often a child can **say** what is expected, but may not be able to **do** it. We have all had the experience of a child who can **tell** us that he should have asked for the toy instead of hitting Billy, but the next time he wants the toy, he hits Billy again. This child would probably say just the right things in a social work discussion group. But watch him in action. We are puzzled because he said he knew what to do, but he did not do it. And you know why. Talking is not everything. Obviously, such a child has a need to hit Billy. This can easily be overlooked in a group based solely on discussion. You will never see what the child really does. All you will see is what he says.

Troubled children often use talking to distract you from seeing what they might actually **do**. Talking is distant from actions; talking is less definite, less intense. In the experience-oriented Theraplay Group, both you and the children will constantly be **demonstrating** messages and needs to each other.

Children over a wide range of ages have a need for these non-verbal messages. However, using Theraplay as the basis for your social work group will be particularly appropriate when you are servicing children with mental or emotional ages between two and seven. (It goes without saying that the chronological ages of these same children might cover a wider range.) For young children who do not have well developed language abilities, Theraplay is highly effective because it is a non-verbal experience.

The Group has a Highly Nurturing Emphasis

We have talked a great deal about nurturing and why it is important. Theraplay almost always means "nurturing." Being in a Theraplay Group means being nurtured. If you are working in special education, there is a greater chance that the children you work with will not have had enough healthy nurturing messages. Many will actually have had a serious lack of nurturing. Why? To their parents, these kids have failed. They have not made the grade. **They are not normal.** They are "slow." Their parents do not want to punish or hurt their children because of this. But the fact that their child is not normal **hurts the parents.** And when you are hurt yourself, it is difficult to give to, or nurture, the one who has "hurt" you. Thus, and sometimes very early in the child's life, the parents may have stopped providing enough nurturing.

Sometimes this has happened for other reasons. Parents may think that all the child needs is more toughening up, more pushing. Perhaps they think their child is slow because they have been too easy on him. May be they should "make" (i.e., "force") their child to do things on his own. Nurturing, so quickly connected to "babying," is the first dimension to go. **But fostering independence does NOT mean withholding nurturing.** When talking with parents, be sure they appreciate the importance of BOTH.

Children need to be nurtured, not as a reward for something they did that met your expectations, but because we all need to be nurtured. Your Theraplay Group is the place this can happen.

As you give to the children through the NO HURTS rule and through all of the warm, intimate, nurturing Theraplay activities, you will become aware of those children who have particular difficulties with nurturing. This can give you a clue to problems at home. Young children who are adamant about their independence and self-sufficiency, who communicate that they do not need or do not want the nurturing you are providing, may have parents who value independence and who are pleased that their child is not as dependent on them as other children of the same age. These parents might have a problem with nurturing and dependency themselves, and so, they have discouraged signs of childishness, fearfulness, dependency, or vulnerability in their children. Sometimes children have to be grown-up because there is no adult available. These children act like little grown-ups. Although they may have difficulty accepting it, THEY NEED NURTURING.

Certainly, Theraplay provides nurturing in obvious and direct ways (i.e., feeding, lotioning). Nurturing your children **now** will allow them to see the classroom and the group as different from home. It will allow them to receive the nurturing that they may not be able to ask for otherwise, or that they may be asking for in inappropriate ways. And even if their home is negative or punitive, your children may gain strength from at least receiving nurturing **somewhere,** for without any, they may be cold, uncaring, non-nurturing people for the rest of their lives.

The Leader Uses Unique Methods of Positive Structuring

Unless you have had special training in therapy with troubled children, you may not have been exposed to a variety of ways to handle their behavior that are at the same time positive, structuring, and playful. The techniques that we have learned from Theraplay can enhance your effectiveness.

The art of Theraplay is characterized by persistent yet wonderfully positive approaches to structuring. When Rubin was beginning her training as a Theraplay therapist, she was told not to use the word "No." This was not easy. Most grown-ups automatically use "No" when they need to tell a child that they did something wrong or that they should modify what they did. If you want an idea of how often you do use "No," run a tape recorder for an hour while you are actively involved with your children. If you use two "No's," it is probably at least one too many!

What is the problem with "No"?

"No" is not **fun.** "No" is what people do when they are teaching, correcting, or rejecting. "No" is generally not playful, and the Theraplay atmosphere is playful. Thus, the correcting or rejecting "No" does not belong in a Theraplay Group. There are ways to turn the word "no" into a game, and this can be a delightfully surprising thing to do at the opportune time. But if a child has done something "wrong," (left your structure, hurt someone, etc.) saying "No" simply tells him that, once again, he has **failed.** In fact, what this clearly tells him is that he has **failed** you. That you cannot accept what he did. "No, don't do that." That is the entire sentence, really. So instead of giving a message of acceptance, you are telling the entire group that they must live up to your expectations, that you can only accept certain behaviors, not all behaviors. Teachers, and sometimes parents, have to say "No." But the Theraplay Group leader should eliminate that word from her vocabulary unless she is going to use it to play with.

How do we structure without saying "no"? There may be a wide variety of ways to do this, and as you gain experience, you will develop your own. But we will describe a few here that we learned from Theraplay. Some may be familiar to social workers, others to early childhood teachers. Or you may say, "Oh, of course, that's so obvious. Why didn't I think of that?"

Physical Touch

Touch is the cornerstone of Theraplay. When a baby or child is doing something undesirable, his mother takes his hand and moves him away from the area, or picks him up, or moves him in some appropriate way. She may talk to him about it at the same time, but she uses touch and physical structuring as the foundation of the message. This is the easiest, quickest, and least disruptive way to structure in your group. You can hold a fidgety child's hand while you are leading the group. Or you can have him hold onto your leg. You can put your arm on his shoulder. If a child moves away to play with his neighbor, you can pick him up and move him to your side. And you can sit him in your lap.

During a game, if you are not sure that a child will not hurt another while he, for example, is passing along a gentle touch, you can hold the hand that is doing the touching. This lets the child know that you are right there with him. You can say something to explain why you are holding his hand: "I'm going to help you be gentle with Tommy."

How simple a way of structuring can you get? Gentle, supportive, physical help, along with some descriptive, non-judgmental statement such as, "You need some help," or "Come sit with me," or "I want you over here with us."

Challenge

This type of structuring is fun and playful. But use it carefully with children who enjoy being challenged because it may frighten away the timid, fearful child. "Bet you can't . . . " characterizes this technique:

"Bet you can't do this without hurting each other."

"You can't pull each other up when we say, 'Go.' No you can't!"

"Now, I don't think you can do this, 'cause it's pretty hard."

Of course, it is your tone of voice that will tell the children that you are being playful rather than deliberately discouraging. If you are truly able to be playful with your children, it will show in your tone of voice.

Challenge is a technique you may use most often if you have a group of older children, since they will be seeking challenge more than young children. When challenged, they will be tempted to "win" over you, and so they will rise to the challenge so they can prove you wrong! They wind up being successful and so are you!

Paradoxical Techniques

This is slightly different from challenge in that you tell the child not to do the exact thing that you want him to do:

"Don't you put that lotion on the end of my nose. Put it anywhere else, but not on my nose."

"Don't give him a pretzel."

"Don't blow that crazy foam. Keep it on your finger, don't blow it away."

This is a technique that you cannot use often, because the child will learn that you really want him to do what you say you do not. But now and then, it can be just the thing to bring a child into your structure in a playful way. For children who are consistently oppositional, this technique can be perfect.

Prediction

This is another variation on the challenge technique. Here you predict that you think a child will do something in hopes that he responds by doing the opposite:

"Now I know Harry. He always starts before we say 'Go.' I think he's going to do it this time, too! What do you think? Yup! We think you're going to pull up before we say, 'Go.' Let's see what happens. Get ready, get set, Go!"

And, what do you know? This time, Harry waits for the cue, and pulls up at the right time. He fooled you! Just what you wanted!

Using Unwanted Behavior

This is an especially characteristic and clever Theraplay technique. Instead of trying to stop an unwanted behavior, quickly modify your game so you can use the behavior. Thus, unwanted behavior becomes wanted behavior! Instead of the child having to be structured, you have restructured your game. Then, you can continue restructuring your game until you have brought the behavior back to where you wanted it in the first place! For children who are used to reprimands and "No's," it will be a new experience for someone to **want** them to continue this behavior.

For example, you start a game of Group Patticake, and Jenny starts smiling mischievously, hitting her neighbors' hands as hard as possible and screaming as loud as she can.

> LEADER: You know what? Let's try that again. We have to try to keep together. Jenny's got a great idea. She was really using her muscles. Hey, everybody got their muscles? Good. 'Cause this time we have to make some **big** patticakes. And everybody got their throat? Yeah? 'Cause this time we say it **big**, too. Like this: PATTI-CAKE, PATTICAKE, BAKER'S MAN. And you have to make some big hits, like Jenny, but you can't hurt

> when you hit. Let's practice if we can make some big claps with our hands without hurting our hands. Ready? Go!...

> Anybody get hurt? OK, then let's do the whole thing real **big**.

Then, the next time around:

> Wow, was that BIG! Everybody OK? Good. Now let's see if we can make the teeniest little patticakes this time. I don't know if we can do it cause it's real hard...

IMPLICATIONS OF THIS ENVIRONMENT FOR THE GROUP

These are only some of the possible ways you can structure without using "No." Feel free to try any new ways you can think of yourself. But as you begin to get used to structuring without correcting, without implying that the children are **wrong**, but with an optimistic, ever persistent and positive tone, you will be creating an accepting, nonpunitive, and upbeat atmosphere. It is easy to see what benefits can come from such an environment. The children's self-esteem can grow. The children will become more confident, braver. If you can accept rather than reject their behaviors, then they will be able to let them out if they need to, and, when they do not need to anymore, they will stop using them. If you can accept the bad parts of your children as well as the good parts, then they can come to see themselves as OK, bad parts as well as good. (Are not all of us part good and part bad?) And because you are so accepting (structuring and accepting together), they may begin to change to please you. They may grow healthier just to be with you in your group, because it **feels** good to be healthy. This is the difference between **pushing** a child to be appropriate, and developing his desire to be healthy and enjoy pleasant interactions with others in his world. Acceptance can help develop relationships; punishment and correcting can cause a person to want to escape from your company. That is the effect it would have on us. How about you?

You have created an environment that is secure, warm, nurturing, accepting, positive, and one in which these messages are demonstrated and not just talked about. What a rich foundation for the development of group cohesion! And with this foundation, what potential for the process that can occur in your group! We have had some surprising experiences in our groups that we attribute to the secure, accepted feeling that the children developed. We will share them here with you.

Rubin was leading a class of preschool children ages three to five. As they did Check-Ups around the circle, they saw that one child (always very wiggly) had a bad scrape. As Rubin lotioned and said how badly that must have hurt, she asked him (they already had suspicions that he was being neglected or abused) what had happened. He quietly said that his mother had hit him. Rubin said it was too bad that he got hurts from his mother, that it was hard that he got hurts from her. The child was relaxed and quiet as she lotioned and said this. Not quite knowing what to do next to demonstrate her concern for his situation, Rubin then opened it up to the group. She asked, "What do you think of this?" It was the first response that surprised her. Another child said, "My mother does that to me, too." So they lotioned that child also. And another child said, "My mama doesn't do that." And others said, "Mamas shouldn't hurt." And they all lotioned the children who were being hurt. What a delight to see this empathy from preschoolers!

Another time, Rubin was leading a class of learning disabled children, aged ten to fourteen. Again, it happened during Check-Ups. She had gone around the entire circle, verbally and visually checking each child to see if he or she was "OK" to play, and everyone was fine. When she got to the last boy, she asked, "Are you OK today?" He said, "I'm not sure." She said, "What's the matter?" He said, "Well, my sister's girlfriend's mother died last night and I'm not sure I'm OK."

Now death is a topic that not everyone wants to get into. And at an earlier time of her life, Rubin may have chosen to slide over that topic by simply acknowledging that this child may not feel like having fun with the class today, but that the group was going to go on. However, she had watched Diane Mirabito in action, taking advantage of any opportunity to pursue topics of concern that were brought up during a Theraplay Group. In fact, she began to realize that some of these topics may never have been brought up at all were it not for the security and acceptance that had developed among the people in the group, leaders included. So it seemed that creating the Theraplay atmosphere, sharing warmth, understanding, acceptance, and caring, allowed the children to bring up very sensitive subjects.

So, this time, Rubin was ready. She commented that when someone dies, you do feel "funny." Then other children joined in with their questions and remembrances about deaths and funerals. One child told what he remembered of a relative's funeral and his story seemed confused and strange. Rubin said that sometimes, when you are young, you do not understand what is happening and you forget some things and remember others. Maybe he could ask another relative who was there about what happened so he could understand it better. Then, another boy said that his mother had died. Other children talked about wakes they had gone to. The entire session was devoted to this discussion, and at the end, they passed around a treat.

So you see how the atmosphere you have created can lead to your group's beginning to benefit from some discussion. Not total discussion, because they will surely continue to need the security of concrete demonstrations of warmth, acceptance, nurturing, etc. But by using the Theraplay atmosphere, your group can develop to the point where you may be able to use other group techniques that were not successful before.

PHILOSOPHY OF CO-LEADING WITH THE CLASSROOM TEACHER

We have seen that, not only Theraplay Groups, but other social work groups in another teacher's classroom can founder if you are not sensitive to the philosophy and goals of your co-leader: the teacher. If the teacher is not comfortable with the way you run the group, you can anticipate problems.

We think that the issue of the teacher's comfort with what you do in the group is paramount to the effectiveness of your group. Remember that this is the **teacher's** room. You are working with her to meet mutual goals for her class. If you are not supporting each other, the teacher is likely to leave the group, and without her, there will be no group. It may take time for a teacher to become comfortable with a Theraplay Group. Even a teacher who is initially skeptical and doubtful can come to value the group if you respect her opinions and use them to decide how to run your group. We have seen this happen.

In order to facilitate this, you may want to "bend" our Theraplay Group rules. Some teachers may feel strongly that you should exclude a particular child if he is continuously causing trouble. Rubin was in just such a situation. She explained to the teacher why it was so important not to exclude anyone, and suggested that they first try some Theraplay techniques to keep him included and bring him into the group structure. The teacher said OK, and they discussed some possible ways to do this. Rubin tried all the ideas, but they did not work. So, in the end, she agreed to exclude the child from the group.

If you and the teacher are to come to a mutual understanding, you must set up a time to meet regularly to discuss what happened in your last group and to plan for your next group. It will be important for both of you to share ideas as to why certain behaviors are occurring, and how you can both be comfortable handling them.

Social workers particularly, by virtue of your goals for children, can easily get into conflicts with the classroom teacher. You often want to provide the children in your classes with a looser, more accepting atmosphere than is typical of school, one in which they can let off steam, let out feelings (both good and bad), one in which the normal pressures are reduced. Rather than trying to teach, you are trying to create an environment conducive to mental health and psycho-social growth. Therefore, you may feel inclined to let up on the structure and accept behaviors and comments that the teacher may not allow. Sometimes, the stricter the teacher, the more you feel the children need this looser time.

You may very well be right that the children would benefit from such an experience. But if the teacher is uncomfortable, conflicts between the two of you will occur. The children will be in the middle, trying to please both of you. If your group puts them in such a bind, how can they possibly benefit from it?

Let us relate a scenario that did actually happen. The Theraplay Group was held in a special education classroom of children ages five to eight. The teacher was pregnant, tired, and thus did not get actively involved in the group. None of the leaders set aside time to discuss the group and what was happening in it. About one month into the school year, the teacher left to have her baby. The substitute who replaced her did not have any background in special education. She had a punitive approach and used fear to structure the class. She did not stay in the group.

Meanwhile, the children, who probably needed as much nurturing as they could possibly get, were falling apart. In the group, they acted out. The substitute who was totally against allowing such behaviors, assigned one child in the class to report to her if any child misbehaved in the group. This child was also to report what the leaders did. No wonder the children were falling apart! They were being torn apart.

Clearly, such a situation is destructive for all concerned, especially for the children who are supposedly benefiting from the group. We include this experience as a warning. Be sensitive to the classroom teacher, listen to her, and make sure she has a say in what happens in the group. If you are flexible, and the teacher is flexible, you can learn a great deal from each other. Only then will everyone profit from the group.

TYPICAL SOCIAL WORK GOALS APPROPRIATE FOR THERAPLAY GROUPS

1. Increasing age-appropriate behavior
2. Increasing healthy peer interactions
3. Improving social functioning
4. Increasing ability to cope with conflicts
5. Increasing self-esteem

Chapter 14

THERAPLAY GROUPS FOR
THE SPEECH/LANGUAGE THERAPIST

Phyllis Rubin

Mothers and fathers play with their babies. Mommy talks to her baby as she changes his diaper, her eyes are wide, her face is animated, in order to attract his attention to her and hold his interest so he will quiet enough for her to change him. Daddy hides behind the teddy bear, popping out from behind it to say "Peekaboo!" In both situations, baby's eyes are drawn to that special face. Baby's gaze is expectant. He smiles when he is spoken to. When his parent stops talking, he either gurgles, babbles in reply, or flaps his arms and legs to start the interaction again. What is he learning? The pragmatics of communication.

Just from these two interactions described, the baby is learning to establish eye contact, to maintain a topic (attend to one thing), to smile, to initiate interactions (arm/leg flapping), and to turn-take (gurgling between parental speech). These are only a few of the early pragmatic behaviors that babies learn through play and pleasant interactions with their parents in the first months and years of their lives. It is through similar playful and pleasant interactions that speech/language therapists can foster the development of the early pragmatic skills which are frequently missing in children who have language disabilities.

Professionals are increasingly working with children in groups. An expanding number of books, articles, and presentations have appeared concerning the importance of focusing on pragmatics, as well as on receptive and expressive language. In Theraplay Groups, you can focus on all of these areas, but especially on pragmatics. These groups are ideal for providing situations that naturally develop social communication. You will not have to "set up" a situation to elicit a desired response. You will not have to use "sabotage" (setting up a pragmatically incorrect situation that hopefully gets the child to communicate so as to right the situation) to produce appropriate pragmatic language. In Theraplay Groups, the situations will happen naturally. When a child is pragmatically inappropriate, his interactions with you and the group will heighten his awareness of the social situation, thus stimulating appropriate communication.

EARLY-DEVELOPING PRAGMATIC SKILLS

Certain early-developing pragmatic skills are naturally a part of a Theraplay-oriented interaction. Thus, in your Theraplay Group, you will not have to necessarily **plan** to address a particular pragmatic skill, but rather the following skills will continually be required throughout any Theraplay Group session simply by virtue of the four Theraplay Group rules. These skills are:

1. Establishing and maintaining eye contact
2. Conversational turn-taking
3. Initiating communication
4. Verbalizing needs and feelings
5. Responding to the communication of others
6. Reflecting reality in what is said
7. Sharing a topic and conversation
8. Making an impact (or asserting)
9. Clarifying misinterpreted messages

If you need to develop goals for your group, any or all of these would be appropriate. And to look at this from the other side, if you have children who have difficulty with these pragmatic skills, a Theraplay Group will be a most appropriate way to promote the development of these skills.

DEVELOPING PRAGMATIC SKILLS
IN A THERAPLAY GROUP

I will describe a variety of children who have some of these difficulties and will show how the activity and the group rules allow these problems to surface so that normal pragmatic communication can be encouraged. As we have said before, it is not just what you say, but what you do, what you communicate non-verbally, that creates an atmosphere of safety, caring, and fun. And it is this atmosphere that provides the incentive for children to try new pragmatic skills.

The Uninvolved/Isolated Child

Our group is beginning Check-Ups. We are going around, one child at a time, checking for hurts. I ask the group to help me check Jody.

RUBIN: Let's take a look at Jody. Is his nose OK?

GROUP: Yeah.

RUBIN: Head?

GROUP: Yeah.

RUBIN: Alright, let's see your hands.

Jody does not respond. His head is bent down and he does not act as though he is being spoken to.

RUBIN: You've gotta put your hands out like this. (demonstrating)

Jody puts his hands out, not looking at my demonstration.

RUBIN: You've got to turn them over.

JODY: (No response. Head still down.)

RUBIN: (explicitly) Turn them **over.** (again demonstrating)

JODY: (turns hands over)

We already see Jody's unresponsive, uninvolved style of interacting. Using a familiar phrase, he is "tuned-out." He does his "own thing," not yours.

RUBIN: No hurts on his hands. Do you have any hurts today?

JODY: No.

RUBIN: Good!

ARTIE: Yes he do! On his foot.

JODY: I don't got no hurt.

ARTIE: Yes you do.

There is obviously a discrepancy. How do you provide the opportunity for both children to learn appropriate language? Check to see what is real. This is a natural occurrence in Theraplay Groups because not only do we talk about hurts, but we always actively check out the children, find the hurts, and involve the tuned-out child in reality.

RUBIN: Well, we better check it out.

And as I begin to untie his shoe, I see a big scratch on Jody's leg.

RUBIN: Oh, on his **leg**. Look! Jody does have a hurt on his **leg**. Jody, you **do** have a hurt!

JODY: You better put some lotion on it.

Because the group **did** this activity and did not simply talk about it, we uncovered Jody's inability to verbalize reality and to be appropriately involved in the group. This was an ongoing problem for Jody. Frequently, his language did not match with what was happening and he easily became socially isolated. But since we nonverbally carried out the NO HURTS rule by physically checking him and caring for the hurt with lotion, **we did not allow him to remain isolated.** The pleasurable lotion helped him enjoy interacting with others (as opposed to avoiding others). This concrete, deliberate activity made him highly aware of the reality on himself, and gave him (and Artie) vocabulary so he could verbalize what was real. For Jody, this was good practice for talking relevantly in social situations.

Next, Jody had to check his neighbor for hurts. He faced him, looked intently at his face, and found a hurt on his nose. He pointed, "Here, he has a hurt on his nose. I gotta get some bandaids."

Tuned in at last!

The Quiet/Timid Child

Jason is a fearful child, often afraid to talk. He did not have his needs met at an early age, and his parents still dominate him, trying to get him to grow up by forcing him into situations that frighten him and by not responding to his discomfort. At the beginning of the year, he used to avoid our Theraplay Group and cling immaturely to his teacher. He did not know that he could make an impact since he was never successful with his parents. Here in the Theraplay Group, we have created a safe, nurturing, responsive environment that will allow Jason to experiment with asserting and initiating.

Blindfold Walk shows how a secure atmosphere can be created in an activity and how a particular game can promote a specific goal: in this case, asserting.

RUBIN: OK, Jason, it's your turn. We're going to cover you up. What do you have to tell your friends so you won't get hurt?

JASON: Don't bump me.

RUBIN: And if we go too fast, what do you have to say?

JASON: Don't go too fast.

RUBIN: OK, we're going to cover you up. Donny, Carl, hold Jason's hands so he feels OK.

Jason is covered with a small blanket over his head. The entire class holds hands in a big circle and the leader guides them slowly around the room. The adult is always in charge of maintaining safety by making sure the children respond to Jason's needs as they walk him around.

RUBIN: Donny, watch for Jason! Is he OK? Make sure he doesn't bump into that chair.

At the end of the trip around the room, Jason is uncovered. It is now important that the children check on him, and that he gives them feedback on the trip.

GROUP: Jason, did we go too fast?

JASON: (timidly) No.

GROUP: Did we bump you?

JASON: (timidly) No.

GROUP: Were you scared?

JASON: (shook his head "no")

Jason is still a quiet, timid child. But through repeated experiences like this one, in a group that listens to him and cares about him, he will continue to build his courage to verbalize his needs and feelings. He will learn that expressing himself is OK.

The Aggressive Child

Mac and Phil demonstrate a problem caused by the inability to assert needs effectively. What this leads to is aggressive behavior that, in this and any case, is an expression of something more than simply wanting to hurt another person. The leader's job is to respond to, or express, what the aggression is about. It almost always will be due to bottled up or repressed feelings about someone other than the person actually hurt, or due to the need for more nurturing and caring. The incident that follows was not connected to any particular activity, but just "happened," as many important interactions in a Theraplay Group "just happen." This shows how following the NO HURTS rule builds feelings of safety, acceptance, and develops assertiveness.

Mac and Phil are sitting next to each other as the group is singing a song. Phil lightly taps Mac on the leg. Mac does not say anything, and instead hits Phil. The leader, Ellen Whelan, sees only this. To her, it looks like unexplained aggression, and she is surprised because Mac is rather stiff and timid. But she does not punish.

WHELAN: Mac, what's the matter? No hitting! What happened?

MAC: (no response)

WHELAN: Mac, you hit Phil. Why?

MAC: (no response)

WHELAN: You hit Phil. Phil, what do you have to tell him if he hits you?

PHIL: Don't hit me, Mac.

WHELAN: Mac, were Phil's feet too close to you?

MAC: (no response)

WHELAN: I think so. I don't know. Mac, you better tell Phil, keep your feet there.

MAC: Keep your feet there.

WHELAN: You're too close to me.

MAC: You're too close to me.

Since the leader did not see what happened, and these were two children with serious language deficits, unable to describe what really happened, she did the next best thing. She validated and verbalized the feelings of **both** children, while at the same time insisting on NO HURTS. Because no hurts were allowed, both children had to practice an appropriate way of verbalizing their needs. Rather than ignore the hitting as a distraction from the activity, she noticed this inappropriate display of aggression and used it to develop the feeling of being in a safe environment. For Mac, this was a critical issue. He had seen violence at home as a result of alcoholism, and had himself been hospitalized for surgery. These are traumatic experiences for children, experiences that can make them feel helpless and victimized. In fact, Mac was socially stiff and suspicious of others. When Whelan insisted on **everyone's** safety in the group, she increased Mac's trust in others and kept him involved in the group games requiring communication. She also gave him permission and encouragement to use asserting words, thereby building his ability to keep himself safe in the future.

The Impulsive/Manipulative Child

Bear with me while I repeat one of our best examples of an impulsive/ manipulative child. Manny is the epitome of such a child: one who is three steps ahead of us; one who seems to run us around in circles; one who is never really WITH us. Both body and mind are in motion: this child is often physically active, and usually talks constantly as well, yet does not respond to the conversation around him. He seems to listen only to his own drummer, and insists that we do the same. There is little mutuality; no balanced conversation. Children like Manny can be very frustrating. Here we see how Manny's manipulative behavior is repeated in the way he communicates.

Tregay was leading her group in a game of Silly Faces. Each person had a turn to create a silly face to "pass around the circle" (each child would make the new face and "give it" to his neighbor). This requires each child to take turns and to join in the game. Manny's problems surfaced immediately in this activity. Here in play, just as in class and at home, he is unresponsive to the group's communication, and tries to change the topic from silly faces to silly noises.

TREGAY: Manny, got a funny face to pass along?

MANNY: Honk, honk.

TREGAY: That's a funny noise. That's a good idea, we'll do that next.

MANNY: No!

TREGAY: Pass me a funny face.

MANNY: Like what? Ah! E-dee-dee-dee!

> TREGAY: That's a noise! Show me. Show me a face!
>
> MANNY: Rrrrrrarr!
>
> GROUP: That's a noise! Pass me a funny face!
>
> MANNY: Like what?

Manny's conversational behavior is identical to his overt behavior in the group. When you start a conversation with him, he virtually ignores your topic with continuous attempts to change the subject. And if he cannot change the subject, he resists responding to yours ("Like what?")! He must learn to share. Learning to share activities — this activity — is the same skill as sharing a conversation or topic.

Children like Manny need nurturing, because they are almost always doing something wrong. Often they have taken on the role of troublemaker, mischief-maker, disrupter, and that is certainly what he has done in this activity. He will need acceptance and caring to counteract his negative image of himself and to help him develop trust, relax, and eventually be able to join in the group's activity. He also needs a great deal of structuring to keep him "sticking together," responding to others, and developing his ability to be fair rather than "hog" the show. STICKING TOGETHER and HAVING FUN will continue to draw him into the game, and keep him interested enough to finally join in the appropriate topic.

> TREGAY: You know what? It's hard for you to think of a funny face. I'm going to take my turn, and you can think about it a little more. After my turn, you can have your turn again.
>
> MANNY: Nah!
>
> TREGAY: Here comes my funny face! (It gets passed around.) OK, I hope Manny has thought of a funny face, cause I want him to have a turn. Manny, do you have a funny face for us?
>
> MANNY: Yup! (He gives a funny face to pass around.)
>
> TREGAY: Good, you got one!

Theraplay involved Manny in the following ways: first we made the play appealing and then set a firm structure that let him know that he had to stick together if he wanted to share in the fun. Here the whole group helped him with the stick together rule, making him feel wanted in the game. When this did not work, **the adult took over,** again setting a firm structure to which he could respond if he wanted to participate. Here is where the "fun" of Theraplay works. This is not schoolwork he **has** to participate in. This is a game we would like him to share with us—we would like him to enjoy. This is something that would be **pleasurable** for him. As you can see, when faced with losing out on the fun, Manny chooses to share the game. He has not been forced, bribed, insulted or embarrassed. The adult told it like it was, stated what was happening, and gave Manny the non-judgmental structuring and acceptance that allowed him to give up his manipulative tricks and join in the fun. Using play as an incentive to get Manny to practice sharing a topic will help generalize this skill into his normal conversation.

A REAL SPEECH/LANGUAGE THERAPLAY GROUP

What does a real Theraplay Group look like? How do you respond when the pragmatic problems come from several children at the same time?

First, you do have to know the children and their individual needs. Obviously, you will not necessarily handle the same behavior in two different children in exactly the same way. They likely are doing the same behavior for two **different** reasons, and **you respond to the reasons, not the behavior.**

Next, although you may be focusing on one specific pragmatic or language concept in an activity, you will do well to respond when any child ventures outside the Theraplay rules of the adult in charge, no hurts, stick together, and have fun. Responding at such times will automatically develop pragmatic skills; not responding may lead to a more narrowly focused, less flexible group atmosphere in which you will miss many **natural** (remember, that's real pragmatics!) opportunities to foster appropriate social communication.

The following is a description of a closing activity that shows many opportunities for learning pragmatic skills. At the end of a group session, we are passing around a good-bye with a handshake and eye contact. Four pragmatic problems surface.

First is the problem of initiating communication. When the good-bye gets to Mac, he is unable to pass it on.

RUBIN: We're all done. Good-bye! (looking at Saul and shaking his hand)

SAUL: Good-bye! (looking at Winnie and shaking her hand)

WINNIE: (turning to Mich and shaking his hand) Good-bye!

MICH: (turning to Mac and shaking his hand) Good-bye!

MAC: (shakes Mich's hand and then sits there, not moving).

Mac needs help to continue the good-bye and initiate an interaction with the next partner. He cannot do this alone. He needs an adult to start him verbalizing. Whelan, his teacher, helps.

TEACHER: Mac, who are you gonna do it to? Who you gonna say good-bye to?

MAC: (gestures to his neighbor)

TEACHER: Good boy! Artie. Right.

MAC: (Still not moving)

TEACHER: Shake his hand. Tell him "bye."

MAC: Good-bye. (finally shakes hands with Artie)

ARTIE: (shaking hands with Whelan) Good-bye.

TEACHER: (shaking hands with Ron) Ron, Good-bye.

RON: (looking straight ahead, shakes Whelan's hand with deliberate disinterest)

Here, the second pragmatic problem surfaces. Ron is avoiding eye contact and looks uninvolved. But actually, Whelan knows why this is happening. Ron is new to the class and has a different language background. This is his first experience in an English speaking environment. He does not yet feel completely safe in the group. He needs gentle involvement to participate and to respond.

TEACHER: Ron, hi!

RON: (still not looking)

TEACHER: (not letting his hand go, and not taking her eyes off him) Ron, hi!

RON: (turning and looking, smiles and waves "hi" in return, showing he understands and has participated)

RON: (turning and shaking Pete's hand) Good-bye!

PETE: (gets Ron's good-bye and turns to shake Tom's hand) Good-bye!

TOM: (turning to Rubin while Pete is saying good-bye) Good-bye!

The next problem: Tom is so intent on taking his turn, he does not give Pete a real chance to **give him** his good-bye.

RUBIN: Wait, you have to get Pete's good-bye first. You have to get Pete's good-bye.

TOM: (turning back to Pete and making relaxed eye contact)

PETE: Good-bye (shaking Tom's hand again)

TOM: (looking straight ahead, and reaching out his hand, shaking Jody's hand instead of mine) Good-bye!

Right after one, comes yet another problem. Tom, who first was so quick to pass on his good-bye that he did not get one from Pete, now is acting disinterested and is not making the appropriate connection (eye contact) as he says good-bye to me. He does not even see whose hand he is shaking. Both his behaviors are two sides of the same coin. He wants to keep both his distance and his control. He is quite the "little adult," and tends to be in control by being subtly manipulative. He keeps his distance by taking turns when **he** wants to, and by not connecting with people through eye contact. However, he does respond to the communication of others, as you can see now.

RUBIN: Ah, ah, ah, with your eyes!

TOM: (looking directly at me and taking my hand) Good-bye.

RUBIN: Good-bye, Tom.

Then Tom reaches out his hand to Jody, on my lap, who has not had a turn.

TOM: Good-bye!

Another problem. Tom is taking charge, "doing my job" as I sometimes tell the children. I take this opportunity to assert that it is my turn, modeling what I hope the children will be able to do in the future.

RUBIN: Hey! It's **my** turn. (taking Tom's hand away from Jody) I have to give a good-bye to Jody. Jody, good-bye. (shaking Jody's hand)

JODY: (looking down at the floor and away from me) Good-bye.

You remember Jody, the isolated, uninvolved child? He is avoiding making eye contact and connecting with me. As before, at the beginning of the group, I do not let him remain uninvolved. I persist in trying to attract his attention by awakening his interest in me. And I persist until I am successful — uniquely characteristic of the Theraplay Group leader.

RUBIN: (holding onto Jody's hand, looking insistently toward
              him, although he is looking elsewhere) Here I am!

JODY: (still looking away) Good-bye. (trying to pull hand
              away)

RUBIN: (not letting go or turning away; staying with Jody to
              attract his attention, hoping he will **feel** my stare, my
              hand in his, and my insistence; continuing to shake
              and look to attract his curiosity about why I was not
              letting go) Here I am!

Jody finally looks up at me and makes eye contact.

RUBIN: Good-bye!

JODY: (maintaining eye contact) Good-bye!

Because of our insistence that these children stick with one another, care for and about each other, respond to each other and to the adults, we can provide a format in which they can develop the pragmatic skills they will need to be capable social communicators.

Chapter 15

CAUTIONS, AND STARTING YOUR GROUP

There are certain essential steps to take before beginning a Theraplay Group. The first is that the leader should have some training in Theraplay, either the introductory course developed by The Theraplay Institute, or the introductory and intermediate workshops in Theraplay Groups with Children. Such courses will provide three essentials for the leader of the group: (1) a thorough grounding in the rationale for the use of Theraplay; (2) the theory and principles underlying the Theraplay technique so that she will be able to answer the "Why's" she will get from other professionals; and (3) an opportunity to experience the Theraplay atmosphere firsthand (a must if the leader is herself to create this atmosphere in her group).

PREPARING YOUR COLLEAGUES

Once trained and ready to start a group of her own, the leader must now prepare her colleagues for this approach.

If you are a teacher and about to lead your own group in your own room, you would do well to tell your principal and supervisor that you are going to use an additional technique in your class. Tell them what it will look like ("We'll be sitting on the rug."), and how it may sound ("We may get louder and louder before we get quieter and quieter!") (Jernberg, personal communication). But assure them that things will not get out of control. (Some principals and supervisors have more concerns about this than do others.) Obviously, if you are new at leading Theraplay Groups, things may not go smoothly at first. It may take time for **you** to feel comfortable when problems surface, and to learn that you can handle them. Therefore, it will be important for your supervisors to know that you are a beginner, so that they will give you time to practice this technique without pressure.

If you are a related service provider (social worker or speech/language therapist, for instance) and a "guest" in the room in which you are leading a group, you will have to prepare the teacher as well as the principal and supervisor.

We have found through the years, that there are certain essentials that must be discussed with either the classroom teacher or the principal or supervisor. In fact, when we have not attended to these essentials, and thus not received the necessary support, our Theraplay Groups have not been successful. Therefore, before you begin your group, arrange informational meetings (individual meetings are best) with any staff people involved to discuss the following issues.

Professional Philosophies Must be Compatible

There are certain key philosophies that are critical if a Theraplay group is to be supported in any given classroom. First, the people involved must understand that PLAY can foster healthy growth and better functioning both **inside** and **outside** the classroom. Most educators will agree with this last statement, but many are not comfortable with play (especially the highly personal, interactive play characteristic of Theraplay) in a **school classroom.** These people may also feel that school is solely for academics and that they do not need to focus on social behavior in their classroom. However, academics and social behavior **are** connected, and a child's social behavior can either positively or negatively affect his ability to perform academically.

For instance, a withdrawn, fearful child who avoids interactions with others will sit quietly at his desk and work, but he may not be able to ask you for help when he needs to. Instead, he may cry, or become more tense when he finds out he completed his work incorrectly. Or maybe he just sits there without completing his work because he knows he cannot do it alone, but cannot ask for help. The controlling child may resist completing his work just to prove that he is in control and not you. A child who is anxious about something may not even have heard the direction you have given the class. His mind is elsewhere. Helping these children improve their social interactions is another approach to helping them achieve academically. Meeting their social/emotional needs in a Theraplay Group can have a positive effect on their learning behavior.

Allowing problems to surface is the second issue with which many teachers may be uncomfortable. They may feel that this cannot foster healthy growth. It is important that they understand that you want problems to surface during the group, rather than stay repressed or under control, and that it is during the surfacing that you and they will see the underlying issues and be able to deal with them. However, in special education classrooms, there may be a reward system or behavior modification program in operation to increase the appropriate behavior of the children. This would work against the purpose of the Theraplay Group—that is, we want problem behaviors to occur so that they can be dealt with. Thus, you must ask teachers who use behavior modification, not to apply it during the Theraplay Group.

Third, teachers may have difficulty reconciling two seemingly contradictory issues: why does Theraplay provide **nurturing** when we all seem to agree that we ultimately want the children to grow up? There is a hierarchy of the essential messages children need if they are to mature in a healthy manner. The **first** is nurturing: the message children need to make them feel special just for themselves, and not because of something they have done well (grades in school) or something they have given to others (gifts, politeness). Children who only feel loved for what they do well, may learn to perform in an empty manner (affect may be lacking or inappropriate). Or conversely, they may have trouble performing (taking tests, answering questions when asked).

Parents of a special child may react to the difficulties their child has with disappointment and rejection, or even disapproval. It may be very difficult for the parents to love such a child unconditionally. And when he gets to school, this is repeated because our training teaches **us** not to love him unconditionally, but only to give him attention and acceptance when he is appropriate, even though the inappropriate may be a call for help: i.e., Will you be there for me even when I show the bad part of myself? If we answer, "Yes," the child will be able to build a sense of trust in us; to develop the healthy, adult/child relationship he was not able to establish at home. He will become more secure in our room, less anxious, and begin to share problems with us. He will know that he can count on us when he needs help. It is with nurturing that he will feel secure enough to grow and mature. If he needs nurturing and does not get it, he will remain anxious and forever seeking attention in inappropriate ways.

Fourth, some teachers may feel that if they have fun with their class they will lose control. They will need to be reassured that this is not the case, and that the adult can have fun and be in charge both at the same time.

Fifth, they must understand the reason for allowing and **accepting** the honest expression of feelings, both negative and positive. Some teachers may be uncomfortable when negative feelings arise about members of the group and especially the adults in the group. They must understand that it does not help these troubled children when we tell them they must cover up their feelings or deny them ("You don't feel that way.") The teachers must also be reassured that, although we will allow the expression of negative feelings, we will not allow children to use them as an excuse for inappropriate behavior or for hurting others.

If after having discussed all these issues with the teacher, there are still questions about the compatibility of philosophies, you might suggest a **trial period** for your Theraplay Group. A trial period (we suggest eight weeks) will either demonstrate how children can be helped with problems, or determine if philosophies continue to be incompatible. In the latter case, you may see some signs that the teacher is uncomfortable. You may hear her tell the children before group to "be good," or she may suggest that a problem child not be nurtured at the end of the session, or you may find that she is applying her behavior modification program to the group. Or she may simply tell you that she feels the group is getting out of hand because the children are not controlled enough. If this cannot be worked out, we suggest discontinuing the group in that room.

The Teacher and the Entire Class Must Participate in the Group

We have found that a key element in developing real change in children and internalizing social behaviors that carry over and are integrated into the child's whole life, is the inclusion of the entire class and the involvement of the teacher as co-leader. Having the entire class participate together in this group carries out the philosophy of establishing a feeling of family and togetherness. This cannot be achieved if one or more children are either deliberately excluded from the group or are unable to participate due to scheduling conflicts. Although the group that is present may develop into a cohesive and supportive unit, this atmosphere may not carry over to the rest of the class since some children have been left out. Deliberately excluding a child from the group (bad behavior, etc.) can destroy the atmosphere in your group. Remember that you want the children to feel accepted, problems and all, and as a result, to feel more secure. When they see a child excluded, it is a clear message that all are **not** fully accepted in your group, and they may wonder if they will be the next to have to leave. This will hardly build feelings of security. Of course, if there should be a time when a child must be removed from the group, remember that it will have an impact.

Now think about the teacher not participating in your group. What will the children think when they see their teacher leave the room during Group, or sit at her desk and do other work? The messages seem clear. "The group is not important to me. The group is not interesting to me. I don't want to be part of the group." The teacher, of course, is always a model for her class, guiding them toward appropriate school behavior. If she tells her class by her actions that the group is not interesting and that she does not want to be a part of it, how can the children whole-heartedly join in the group? We might predict that the children will begin to tell you that they do not want to be in the group today because, for instance, they have to finish their math work. Like teacher, like children.

Goals Should be Compatible with Classroom Needs

A good way to set the foundation for your group is for you and the teacher to set goals for the group. It is important for her to feel that the group supports her and furthers her objectives for her class, and thus the goals for the group should come primarily from her. Rubin generally asks the teacher what she feels her children need to learn socially and communicatively. What do they need to learn to get along better with each other and in school—not academically, but interactively? The teacher may need time to think about this. Some teachers can recognize this area of need in their children more easily than others. If they do not have a feeling for this area at all, you may ask some questions about their children:

1. When they need help with something, can they ask for it?
2. When they need to be assertive, are they?
3. Do they show caring for their peers?
4. Do they express their feelings appropriately and constructively?

Time Must be Allowed for Conferencing

Because of the importance of the teacher's role in carrying out Theraplay principles in the classroom, it is essential that time be allotted for communication between the therapist and the teacher.

Why do we insist on this conferencing between co-leaders? If you are leading a group in someone else's room, conferencing can make or break your group. Now, obviously, if you and the teacher are in perfect harmony, "on the same wave length" in terms of the Theraplay philosophy, you may only be comparing notes about the last session and sharing ideas for up-coming sessions. With this teacher, your group will probably not break down. However, with someone not fully aware of, or comfortable with, the Theraplay philosophy, there are likely — this is important to remember — **very likely** to be areas of conflict that arise during the group. The teacher may not agree with the particular way you handled a child, but will not tell you this without an opportunity. She may very well know this child better than you, and have an idea of why he behaved strangely during a session which could signal the need for a different way of responding to him. It is to **your** benefit to know this. If she is silently opposing you, it will show eventually in any number of ways that are sure to decrease the effectiveness of your group. Certainly there will be little, if any, carryover when you are not there. The children will begin to get subtle messages that you and their teacher disagree.

Rubin is continually surprised when she conferences with teachers and aides. New information always comes out. It may be something Rubin never knew about a child. Or the teacher tells her about something in a child's life or family, wondering if that could have something to do with the trouble he is having in the group. Or, by listening to the questions and comments, Rubin realizes the teacher does not understand something that has been done in the group. Maybe the teacher will say she was uncomfortable with an activity, or with the way her class responded, or that she was getting angry at a particular child and maybe thinks another adult should sit next to him. Or the aide could react this way also. We cannot say this too often: YOU NEED TO KNOW THIS. You may not want to know that others disagree, but talking about it is the first step toward any compromise or understanding. Not talking about it will lead to a "divorce" between the co-leaders ("parents") and leave guilty children ("class").

PREPARING YOURSELF

You have the potential of building a very special relationship with your group. In this relationship, as in any other, you must be aware of the possibility of transference and countertransference. This is not something that occurs only in psychotherapy. It can happen in parent/child relationships, husband/wife relationships, and yes, teacher/student relationships. Countertransference simply means that you do to the child what was done to you as a child, or that you see the child as yourself and give to him what you wished you had gotten from your parents (Jernberg, 1979, pg. 431). By doing so, you are giving to yourself. You are meeting YOUR needs, not the child's. It is a common phenomenon.

It is important that you realize this can happen, and that it may not be good for the children or for you if it does. There are steps you can, and should, take to guard against this.

First, carefully plan the activities for your Theraplay Group. This will give you time to sit back, think about the child's needs and how they can be met, rather than leaving you susceptible to the pull of your own needs during Group.

Second, ask yourself, "Why am I choosing **this** particular activity, and why **now**?" (Jernberg, 1979, pg. 432) Answering this question will help you to further differentiate your needs from those of your group.

Third, videotape your sessions and review them later. You may be surprised by what you see yourself do. You can also get a different perspective on the children. This may lead you to question the reasons for some of your responses.

Fourth, arrange for supervision. There are many ways you can do this. There may be a colleague, social worker, psychologist, etc., in your setting who would be willing to work with you. Your setting may provide support supervision or counseling, or you can bring this up with your own therapist if you have one. If you want formal training and supervision, this can be arranged through The Theraplay Institute, or the authors. Long-distance supervision (using videotapes) is available.

HOW TO START LEADING A THERAPLAY GROUP

You have now set the groundwork. You are ready to actually start your group. However, whether or not you have had the benefit of Theraplay Group training, and assuming you are not working with a Theraplay therapist, we have some suggestions for you as you begin trying to lead your Theraplay Group. This will not be easy. The following ideas are given with those difficulties in mind.

1. If you have more than one group or class with which you could lead

a Theraplay Group, pick the least troubled group to start with. The reason is obvious. There is so much new for you to attend to and learn, it will be all the harder if you have to learn with your most disturbed children. It will be better if there are fewer demands on you.

2. It will help if you develop a clear goal for your group. It could help you remember what you are hoping the children will gain from your group. It will give you a sense of direction and will give your group continuity. You will also have a means to assess the group's progress. Remember, simple, general goals are best.

3. To repeat: Do not include your group in any behavior modification program that may be used in your room. Remember that rewards for "good" behavior will serve to repress needs that may only be able to be expressed through "bad" behavior. If you really want needs to surface, you must not reward and punish. You must try to be supportive and accepting of both appropriate and inappropriate behavior.

4. When you start your group, DO NOT TEACH ANYTHING! Forget your newly written goals. If you do not, you will probably come off as expecting the children to give you the "right" response, to "do it right." **You** will also probably be intent on completing the activity and "doing it right." Actually, THIS IS A NATURAL TENDENCY, AND ONE THAT EACH NEW TRAINEE HAS FELT. So, what we are suggesting is probably going against your natural grain. You will probably feel an urgency for the group to get the games "right," to behave appropriately, to finish all you had planned for the session. When this does not happen, you will feel that you are failing at leading your group. BUT YOU AREN'T! You are just trying to repeat in the Theraplay Group what you have been trained to do. Have patience with **yourself.** You are learning something entirely new.

Here it is not really important to finish all of your planned activities for the session. It is not important to finish even one. It **is** important to respond to the needs of your children. To do that, you first must practice freeing yourself to HAVE FUN and be responsive to the children, rather than your lesson plan!

Instead of trying to accomplish something, HAVE PURE FUN! Fun for fun's sake, not for learning. At this point, if you try to make it for learning, it is likely not to be fun anymore. This will eventually change. But the first and foremost thing for YOU and the group to experience is a shift in the focus from learning and "doing things right," to just enjoying yourselves and having fun together.

5. To help you HAVE FUN, pick non-challenging, well-structured games for your first sessions. Deliberate, one-at-a-time activities may be best, such as Pass-it-Along, Partner Pull-Ups, Check-Ups, and Group Patticake. Hopefully, this will help keep the group sticking together and focused, and will free you up to have fun.

6. As you continue your sessions, you may find that you are having so much fun that you are becoming somewhat uncomfortable because the level of excitement or stimulation is getting too high. If you are feeling uncomfortable, try providing more structure in the sessions. You can do this in a number of different ways. Slow the pace of the games. Have the children restate the structure that you have given them. Make sure they follow through using all the positively structuring techniques we talked about in Chapter 13.

Now you are balancing the elements of structure and fun.

7. If you have not done so already, it is time to add deliberately nurturing activities to your session. Also, pay more attention to signs that the children may need nurturing. If a child minimizes something unpleasant or a hurt, resist your temptation to agree that it was no big deal. Make it a big deal. Take it as a sign that he has learned to deny his need for nurturing, and practice positive, insistent, yet gentle ways to get around his resistance. **You** respond in the way he should have responded. In a way, you are practicing "babying" the children more. To help, try lotioning, smelling lotion on each other, fixing hurts, feeding, and singing songs.

Now you are balancing structure, nurturing, and fun. One more to go.

8. When you feel comfortable with that bunch of elements, you can add challenging activities. Since you are encouraging the children to be braver, stronger, more independent and competent, these tend to create more excitement, and with it, reduce structure. Such activities are Touch Blue, Blindfold Friend Guess, Run To Us, Pass the Ball, Cross-over Dodgeball, Beach Ball Roll, and Tunnel. If things should get out of hand, you can always add more structure. Another way to try challenging games is to take a less challenging one and modify it to create more challenge. This can often be done by allowing the children more space and freedom with which to do the activity, speeding up the activity, encouraging them to do something harder or louder or to use words rather than actions or gestures. If the group still gets out of hand, do not worry. Maybe it is not you who was not ready for challenge; maybe it was the children. Go back to structure and nurturing.

You have now tried all four Theraplay elements. Remember, achieving a natural balance between nurturing, structure, challenge, and fun (stimulation) is the key to a successful Theraplay Group. This takes time. For our trainees, it took about one year for them to feel comfortable with their own style of leading a Theraplay Group and comfortable that they could be responsive to the needs of their children. So take your time and do not be discouraged.

9. Use your co-leader to help you be aware of needs around your group. You will feel that everything is happening at the same time. While you are doing something with one child, a child across the circle is having trouble. You may not even realize this, especially when you are new at leading a Theraplay Group, or even when you become an old hand. Tell your co-leader to tell you **right in the group** that so-and-so is having trouble. Then you can tell her to hold his hand, or sit him in her lap. You may at first feel that you yourself should handle each and every problem. It will take time for you to learn how to balance your handling the problems, asking your co-leader to handle problems, and sometimes choosing to ignore some problems while at other times opening up a problem to the whole group and focusing on it for the rest of the session.

More balancing!

At this point, if you like it, keep at it. We did not say it would be easy. But once you get the hang of it, you will begin to enjoy the many benefits and great potential the group can offer you. Your children will ask for the group if you forget or stop doing it. As a matter of fact, they will most likely ask for extra sessions.

And whereas the unfamiliar observer would say that the children want Group because it is play, you know now that your children want it for reasons much deeper, but which they would not be able to express. A Theraplay Group does something for the child's inner self as well as his outer self in relation to his peers and his teacher. It develops a feeling of connectedness among the group members, and allows the individuals to interact and grow with each other. As you learn to lead the group, you, too, will also grow. It can be a profound experience for all, one that allows us to touch a part of ourselves that is easily submerged and forgotten with today's goal-oriented, academic-achievement focus. It is an experience that all of you will be able to take with you and build upon throughout the rest of your lives.

Chapter 16

TRIED-AND-TRUE THERAPLAY ACTIVITIES FOR THE CLASSROOM

This is a compilation of activities that have been used successfully with the classes we have talked about in this book. If your children are developmentally delayed, you will want to pick activities based on their developmental ages rather than chronological ages. Also consider your children's emotional ages. Often children who are behaviorally or emotionally disturbed will not have an intellectual delay, but an emotional delay, and this is the age to consider when picking activities. Whether or not there are delays involved, most activities can be adapted to appeal to the children you are working with.

We begin with activities for all ages, continue with those appropriate for preschoolers, with the activities becoming progressively more challenging. The first section contains activities that we have used in special education classrooms with approximately ten children. With some modifications, they can be suitable for larger groups. The last section contains activities, developed by kindergarten teacher, Mary Alice DaCosse, that are ideal for large groups as well as small. If you have a small group, be sure not to bypass this section. Hers are some of the most appealing and creative games we have ever seen.

Each activity provides different combinations of the Theraplay elements of nurturing, stimulation, structure, challenge. You will need to judge whether an activity is appropriate for your group. As we have mentioned elsewhere in this book, you can modify these activities so that they focus on the particular messages that your group needs. Also, you can always adjust activities so that they are comfortable for you.

SUCCESSFUL SMALL GROUP ACTIVITIES

Opening Songs

"Where oh Where?"—To the tune of "10 Little Indians"

Where oh where is our friend _____?
Where oh where is our friend _____?
Where oh where is our friend _____?
. . . (Child peeks and says, "Here I am!")

Since this resembles the game of Peekaboo, this song is best for pre-school children. If your children are at the younger end, each child (at his turn) can be given a scarf, blanket, or towel to drape over his head. This seems easier for them to do than holding their hands over their faces. At the pause, the child can pull the blanket off and say, "Here I am!" Variations: Children do not hide, but watch as the leader looks for each child in a pant leg, behind other children, etc., until the child says, "Here!"

"We Welcome"—to tune of "We Wish You A Merry Christmas" (Jernberg, pg. 131)

We welcome our good friend _____.
We welcome our good friend _____.
We welcome our good friend _____.
And we like his _____.
(or And he looks so happy)

A member, or the whole group, decides on something special, new, or important to say to recognize each person that day.

Closing Songs

"The More We Get Together"

The more we get together, together, together.
The more we get together, the happier we'll be.
Cause your friends are my friends,
And my friends are your friends.
The more we get together, the happier we'll be.

"I Like to Play with You" (Make up your own tune as Phyllis Rubin did)

I like to play with you. (or: We like to play together)
I like to play with you.
Today we **ACTIVITY #1** (played patticake),
And then we **ACTIVITY #2** (ate pretzels).
And now we're singing a song.
And we had fun.
I like to play with you.

"Twinkle-Twinkle Little Star"

Twinkle, twinkle little star.
Oh, what special kids you are.
Nice brown (soft, shiny, etc.) hair
Nice soft cheeks
Big bright eyes from which you peek
Twinkle, twinkle little star.
Oh, what special kids you are.

"Bingo"

I know a farmer had a dog
And Bingo was his name-O
B–I–N–G–O
B–I–N–G–O
B–I–N–G–O
And Bingo was his name.

"If You're Happy and You Know It"

If you're happy and you know it **clap your hands.**
If you're happy and you know it **clap your hands.**
If you're happy and you know it
Then your face will surely show it
If you're happy and you know it **clap your hands.**
(Each person says a different thing to do)

If the group or a member has reason to be mad about something, you can sing, "If You're Mad and You Know It," and make an appropriate (for school) gesture (mad face, stamp feet, make a fist, say "I'm mad"). Other feelings can be used also: "If you're sad and you know it . . ."

Games for All Ages

Check-Ups or **Fixing Hurts**

This is a way to say "Hi" to each child as a special welcome. Each child gets checked out by the group to see if he still is the same child he was last session and if he has brought with him all his special "things": fingers, nose, blue eyes, loose tooth, etc! "OK, Jimmy gets a big hello! Hi, Jimmy, welcome back today. We're glad you're here. Let's see how you look. Hey, you've still got your big brown eyes, and those long eyelashes. Still got your feet and toes? Yup. Good. Oh boy, and your smile, you brought it back! I love it. Looks like you're ready to play."

Along with acknowledging each child, you can also spend some time seeing if each child has any hurts to be "fixed" with some lotion or powder around it (not on it — it is not medicine). If a child does not have a hurt, the group can give him a congratulatory cheer and he can pick the body part on which he would like some powder or lotion.

In a beginning group, the adults should be the nurturers. Later on in the life of the group, each child can check his neighbor for hurts and do the nurturing with supervision. If a child often comes with more than his fair share of hurts, the adult should show real concern, telling the child and group that she will check the hurts next week to see if they are better, that this child brings too many hurts and maybe he might try not to bring so many next time. During the next session, remember to count the hurts to see if there are less of them. In an established group, the children can begin to relate how they got the hurts. Bring lots of empathy.

Beach Ball Name Game

This is a good game for new groups that can get progressively harder and more challenging. Initially, it can be used as an opening game, good for getting-to-know each other. A sponge ball is passed from person to person, but the passer must first say the catcher's name **before** passing. To get harder, instead of calling out the catcher's name, the passer must now describe something about the person. Each time the game is played the group could try giving different descriptions of each person: Type of hair; color of hair; description of clothes or shoes; favorite things to do; favorite foods (these last two would have to have been discussed at a previous time). For older groups, pass an imaginary ball that each child can change into whatever he likes (watermelon, fish, T.V., teacher, etc.)!

Do the throw and catch match up to what the imaginary object is? (Orlick, 1982, pg. 59)

Partner Stand-Ups and Sit-Downs

Partners sit on the floor, hold hands, and touch toes together. Then someone (one of them, or the whole group watching) counts, "1-2-3-Go." On "Go," the partners pull up and stand **at the same time** so that neither falls and both get pulled up. Cooperation is necessary to be successful. This can be reversed by beginning in a standing position while touching toes and holding hands, and then sitting down on the count of 1-2-3-Go. For older groups that have been successful in pairs, challenge them by trying a 3-person stand-up. Key: **Toes together,** simultaneous, balanced, cooperative pulling up. Also, older kids can try stand-ups with backs together and elbows linked. Hard! How many people can stand up together in your group? (Orlick, 1978, pg. 31)

One Potato-Two Potato

Everyone sits in a circle and you pass a ball (balloon, towel, kleenex, etc.) around and sing "1 potato—2 potato—3 potato—4 . . . 5 potato—6 potato—7 potato—MORE!" Whoever has the ball on "MORE" gets a variety (depending on the set-up of this particular game) of surprises: A tickle (soft and gentle, please) by as many of the group as possible. **Be careful** because a tickle can easily turn into an attack that can be more sadistic than pleasant (Jernberg, personal communication). To prevent this from occurring, the surprise can be a tickle given by the "MORE's" two neighbors rather than the entire group. Or a pretzel given by a neighbor, or a hug given by the two neighbors. What other surprises can you come up with?

Again, take special care that this is kept at a pleasant level under the tolerance of the child receiving the surprise. Tregay suggests, in fact, calling it a "soft surprise" and emphasizing the gentleness of the interaction.

Balloon Balance

Partners must balance a balloon, beach ball, or foam ball between them without using their hands and while walking. Try using stomachs, upper arms, foreheads, backs, chins. Sophisticated groups can try with more people or more balloons or both! Hard, fun, but can get wild. Keep calm! (Orlick, 1978, pg. 17)

Crazy Foam Play

Crazy foam is aerated foamy soap that looks like shaving cream but feels like a puff of bubbles. We found it in toy stores. We recommend the white kind, since colored foam stains hands and clothes until they are washed. No matter their ages, all people (adults included) are amused and intrigued by crazy foam games.

The first time this is introduced to the children, they might simply want to feel and "shmush" it. Then you can put a ball of foam on your finger and blow it to your neighbor (or his tummy, knee, nose, hair, etc.). Usually when playing this game, we include the structure of, "Get ready, get set, go!" Then you can pass it by "squooshing" it from chin to chin, cheek to cheek, etc. (No hands, please!), around the circle, or encourage independent thinking by having each person pass it to a different part of his neighbor. At the end, you can put the foam in your hands and all clap to make snow. This game is just "PURE FUN."

Pass-It-On

This is a good getting-to-know-you activity for new groups, getting them used to touching each other, and getting touched, **gently.** The leader touches his neighbor in a special way (a soft tickle for his ear, a wiggle for his nose, a hug, a kiss, a rub, etc.) or gives him something gentle (lotion, powder, treat, etc.), and this is passed around the circle until it comes back to the leader. Each person can have a turn to be the leader when you want to encourage independent thinking.

For older children, ages nine and up, we have played **Cumulative Pass-it-Along.** The leader passes one touch to his neighbor who passes both it and a new touch to his neighbor, and on it goes around the circle. The number of touches passed increases each time, and at the end, the leader gets back all the touches that everyone has passed along. (Brody, pg. 29)

Lotion Body Part Pass

The leader puts lotion on any of her body parts (elbow, chin, ear, nose, etc.). She passes it to her neighbor by rubbing it off her nose, for example, and onto her neighbor's nose, and so on around the circle. If someone runs out of lotion, put more lotion on his body part so the passing can continue. People are always amused by this one! It is a playful way to get nurtured.

Pillow Smash or **Pillow Throw**

This is a very handy activity when the entire group or the majority of its members is upset and anxious about something and you cannot settle them down to do any other activity. The leader takes a small pillow (or anything good to hit), and while hitting it with her fist, says something that she is mad about. The pillow gets passed around the circle. This can be modified by each person throwing it to another member of the group, the thrower saying, "I'm mad because we didn't get to play a game." If the group is significantly anxious, just this pillow game, followed by nurturing activities like treats, will be enough for the session.

Food Share

This is a good closing activity along with singing a song. Each person feeds his neighbor a treat—i.e., pretzels, raisins, chips, etc. Very young children will need help and modeling to feed the treat into their neighbor's mouth without eating it first! It helps for the leader to start the feeding so that each child has gotten his treat before he is asked to give one to his neighbor. The eater must also allow himself to be fed. This way, all get and give nurturing. Eye contact and caring should be promoted. Use your imagination to modify this activity to meet your needs, taking into account the ages of your children and their social development as they progress through the year.

1. You can put the treat on various body parts (fingers, shoulders, knees, chins) for neighbors to eat it without using their hands. At first, young children may all go around the circle using the same body part. Later, to foster creative and independent thinking, and as a challenge to older groups, each person could pick another body part on which to put the treat.
2. Raisins can be stuck onto various body parts and eaten off.
3. Older children, with an expected age-appropriate resistance to body contact and to feeding each other, can throw—GENTLY— raisins or rounded pretzels into their neighbor's mouth. Or they can give their neighbor a pretzel in his hand. Do not try to force this regressive type of activity on teens or preteens. Always modify your activities so children can be nurtured in an appropriate way for their age.
4. More sophisticated groups can actually pass around the bag of

pretzels, each offering his neighbor a treat which the neighbor eats himself.

5. Older children love to put treats on various parts of their own bodies and try to eat the treat themselves. Sometimes they make designs on their faces with pretzels. Pictures can be taken of their creations.

Preschool to Teenage Games

Silly Bones

This can be a partner or circle game. Partners must touch their hands (ears, elbows, knees, feet, noses, etc.) together on cue. For older children, they can add new touches while keeping the old ones! Young children in a circle can pass around an elbow (ear, etc.) touch, one-at-a-time, to each neighbor until it gets back to the starter. A small group can attempt for everyone to touch at once, but probably only certain body parts like heads, arms, elbows, big toes, shoulders, pinky fingers. This does sound like fun and good picture material. (Orlick, 1978, pg. 43)

Row-Row and Group Row-Row

Partners sit facing each other with legs straddling the other's legs and holding hands. One lies down and they take turns pulling each other up into a sitting position as they sing "Row-Row-Row Your Boat." One child at a time can be added to each side of the boat, until the whole class is rowing a giant boat. Adults may have to help each side take turns going up and down. Make sure all holds are gentle and that nobody gets pulled too hard.

Tunnel

The children make a tunnel with their hands and feet (or knees) on the rug and their bodies arched in the middle for one classmate to crawl through.

Group Patticake

Because it is more challenging than the typical two-person Patticake, it is a good structuring activity for five and six year olds as well as for preschoolers.

The class sits in a circle. Each person holds up his hands so that his right hand is clapping his neighbor's left, and his left hand is clapping his other neighbor's right.

All together as you clap, you also chant:

Patticake-patticake baker's man.
Bake me a cake as fast as you can.

(Now hold hands with partners and make a circular motion:)

Roll it

(Now clap again:)

And pat it,
And mark it with a "K."
And put it in the oven for us today!
    (or: the kids today)
    (or: the Group today)

(Everyone can "put" a gentle tickle in his neighbor's tummy.)

Hand Prints

Gently rub powder on a neighbor's hand and help the child press his hand on dark construction paper to make a print. You can also make nose, chin, elbow, etc. prints. Try to get all prints on one piece of paper for display. Can each child remember which print is his, hers, or whose? (Jernberg, 1979, pg. 117)

Ring-Around-a-Rosie

The usual game with the children falling down **gently**. This is a game for your youngest or most delayed children. Even a class of autistic children loved this.

Group or Partner Rock-a-bye

This is modeled after the individual Theraplay activity of cradling a child and singing him a song. The group sits in a straight line, each child next to the other. One child lies down across all the laps, and the group sings to him. Each child has a turn.

To do this with partners, each child gets a turn to cradle the other, while the whole group sings together. Rock-a-bye Baby has a unique Theraplay twist:

Rock-a-bye (____), on the tree top.
When the wind blows, the cradle will rock.

When the bough breaks, the cradle will fall
And we will catch (_____), cradle and all.

Train

The group sits in line, each person in back of the other, with legs straddling the child in front and arms around his waist. The first person (teacher, or maybe a child) is the engine; the last is the caboose. They all try to move the train by shuffling on legs and bottoms, around curves, into stations, whatever your imagination and the room allows. (Brody, pg. 30)

Toesies

Partners lie down with feet or toes touching and try to roll across the rug without breaking their "toe-hold." Try this with other body parts touching. (Orlick, 1978, pg. 17)

Making a Christmas Tree

At Christmas time, we tried this activity to give one child a chance to feel special. He was made the group Christmas tree. He got in the center of the circle, and the rest of the group adorned him with pretend Christmas tree ornaments. Then we all admired him. This activity may be modified for other holidays also.

Walk Around the Circle Hug

While everyone sits in a circle, two partners try to walk around the circle while hugging each other. Naturally, you can increase the number of children hugging until the entire group tries to maneuver around the area in a giant hug! Leaders, don't forget to have your turn!

Hot Dog Wrap

The children turn their backs to the middle of the circle. The adult picks one child to be wrapped in a blanket or large towel. Others turn around and guess who is the "hot dog." Then he gets gently unwrapped and "found."

Wrap Up Present

This is similar to Hot Dog Wrap, but the children do not "hide their eyes." Everyone watches while one child gets wrapped up in a large sheet or light blanket. A pretend ribbon can be tied around the package. Then the group can open it up, delighting in the special present inside.

Scotch Stick

Using a piece of scotch tape or masking tape, each person sticks the tape onto a body part of his neighbor. The tape is passed around the circle. Sounds simple, but little kids get a kick out of it. (Orlick, 1982, pg. 33)

Walking with a String

Partners must either hold the ends of a small piece of string, or each must keep a finger stuck to a piece of tape, and walk around the group circle without letting go or coming unstuck! This fosters awareness of working with a partner. For successful partners, increase the challenge by adding a third person to the string- or tape-holding group. You can easily spot the children who walk as though they are the only ones holding onto the string! (Orlick, 1982, pg. 27)

Duck-Duck-Goose Hug

The children sit in a circle. With very young children, adults may need to stay outside the circle to direct the game. Each child has a turn to do the usual "duck-duck-goose," with pats on the head around the circle. When the "goose" is picked, he runs in one direction around circle, and the first child runs the other way. When they meet, they hug **gently**. (Brody, pg. 30)

Cotton Ball Tickles

One cotton ball is passed around the circle. The child who is to be tickled can close his eyes and guess (feel) where his neighbor has touched him gently with the cotton ball. This can also be done with eyes open, so the child just enjoys the pleasant feel of the tickle.

Wheel-Barrel Walk

Be sure you have a soft floor covering to do this game. Children can divide into partners, or each child can have his turn with one of the adults. One child gets on hands and knees. His partner (or the adult) takes a hold of his ankles, and carefully and slowly lifts the first child's legs off of the floor. Then the child must walk on his hands, while his partner follows him from behind, holding his legs. The partners can go from one side of the group area to the other, while the rest of the group cheers them on. (Jernberg, 1979. pg. 123)

Run to Us

Half of the group is on one side of the group area with an adult. The other half is on the other side. One-by-one, each child has a turn to run, on cue, to the other side. To get ready for the runner, the "catching" side holds hands and forms a large semicircle. Then they say together, "Get ready, get set, GO!" When the runner runs, the group surrounds him in a giant hug. Then it is the turn of someone on the catching team to be the runner. Everyone must have a turn, of course. As with all games, if the groups can handle it, the leaders should also have a turn to run and be "caught."

People Roll

The children lie on their stomachs on the rug, side by side. One at a time, each child has a turn to roll over the "logs" of people with adult help. The rollers should lie parallel to the "logs" and roll gently! (Fluegelman, 1976, pg. 117)

Shape/Color Matching

Cut pairs or triplets of squares, circles, triangles, etc. in the same color, or use the same shapes in different colors. Have just enough, or one extra, of the cut-outs for all the people in the group. Lay the shapes in the middle of the circle on the floor. The group stands up, holds hands, and walks around in a circle to a record or while singing a song. At the end of the song, each child must pick up a shape (or color) and find his "partner(s)" with the same shape (or color) and then hug together. This adds a bit of conceptual learning to a challenging and nurturing game. (Orlick, 1982, pg. 41)

Group or Individual "Sandwich"

This is OK for a **small** group of **small** children. The group is challenged to make a sandwich and each child decides what he wants to be (i.e. bread, mustard, ham, pickle). As each decides, he lies on top of the others on the rug or mat. Adults can "eat" them up or peel off layers one at a time.

For Individual "Sandwich," one child decides what kind of food he wants to be: i.e., a pizza, cake, or some type of sandwich. He lays on the floor in the middle of the circle. The group decides what to put on him (pizza sauce, cheese, pepper, etc.), and then all pretend to eat him up. (Orlick, 1978, pg. 35)

Shoe Find

The group sits in circle. The first time this game is played everyone takes off **one** shoe, and all shoes are put in the middle of the circle. The adult mixes them up. Everyone closes his eyes and picks a shoe—hopefully one belonging to someone else. Everyone opens his eyes and guesses whose shoe he has and gives it back to the owner. Watch out for kids who just have to pick their own shoe! Then you can try finding two shoes at a time. This game gets better the larger the group.

Circle Ball Pass

This is a good game for beginning groups and young groups, but there are creative ways to make it more challenging for older groups as well. The children sit close together in a circle. Pass the ball around in various ways—first a regular hand pass, then rolling it over your neighbor's outstretched legs, rolling into his lap, using different body parts to do the rolling, etc. Older groups can try rolling it to neighbors without using their hands, just legs! (Orlick, 1982, pg. 43)

Brown-Skin Day

This was a game we created for a class which seemed to be dividing into racial groups. We announced in the group that this was Brown-Skin Day. We looked for brown skin, felt its softness, and lotioned it. Some people had more than others. Some had very little or none at all. Freckles, moles, etc., even scars were brown skin that received our interest, appreciation, and nurturing. Certainly this can be done, with sensitivity, for any color of skin or physical difference. We think that this type of activity can allow the leader to show her appreciation of such characteristics, and serve as an important model for the rest of the class. Such experiences could prevent alienation between subgroups within the class.

Powder or **Lotion Guess**

One child closes his eyes, or is blindfolded. His neighbor picks either powder, lotion, crazy foam, etc. to put on his hand. The first child must guess, without smelling, what was put on him.

Ball and Blanket

The children sit in circle and hold an edge of a large towel or small blanket. The leader starts a foam ball or beach ball rolling in a direction.

1. Call out someone's name and all must help in getting the ball roll to that person.
2. Describe a person and get the ball to roll to that person.
3. All try to roll the ball from neighbor to neighbor around the edge of the blanket.
4. All stand up and try to throw the ball in the air and catch it in the blanket. This can easily get too wild since the balls move around. You may be able to try this sitting down with the goal of throwing the ball in the air carefully enough for it to land back in the blanket. Everyone really has to work together to accomplish this. (Orlick, 1982, pg. 221)

Blindfold Walk

One child is blindfolded—putting a towel over his head is good—and the group holds hands together and with him and slowly walks him around the room being reminded to be careful for the blindfolded child so he does not hurt himself or bump anything. This game not only gets the helpers to be concerned for the blind child's safety, but the blind child can express his needs to his helpers, such "Not so fast, cause it makes me scared." The helpers must be responsive to the "blind" child. (Orlick, 1978, pg. 27)

Follow the Leader

This game is most often played sitting in a circle, but if you have a good group, you can stand up and play the real game. It can be a good game for structure and for practicing asserting, and it gives the children a chance to take different roles. Each person has a turn to be "leader," picking an action for all the others to do along with him. The child/leader can announce or demonstrate the action, and then give the direction, "One, two, three, GO!" (or "Get ready, get set, GO!) He can be encouraged to watch for children who may not follow his direction or his action, and helped to assert the direction again. The "leader" should also tell the group when to "STOP!" and make sure everyone listened.

Depending on the size of your group, you may not be able to give all the children a turn to be leader in one session. We did this activity across many sessions, keeping a list of who had had a turn, and giving two people a turn in each session until everyone had been leader. Plan ahead to make sure you have enough time, or enough sessions, to give each child a turn. (Brody, pg. 29)

Partner Body Check

This is a relaxing, nurturing, yet somewhat challenging activity that heightens the children's awareness of their classmates. Each person must feel his neighbor's hand (nose, cheek, chin, ear, etc.) and tell if it is warm or cold. This is good for children who need help focusing on reality and therefore is excellent for development of functional language.

Talking Through a Balloon

The leader starts by holding a balloon against the ear of her neighbor, and whispering, or talking very softly into the balloon. The neighbor then does the same thing to his neighbor, passing around the message in this fun way. Be sure the children remember to talk very softly since the sound is amplified through the balloon.

Guess Who's Hugging You

This is a game for children who may have trouble accepting a face-to-face hug from a peer. Each person gets a turn to get covered up with a blanket. Another child is picked to give him a hug, and then the covered child tries to guess who hugged him. The focus should be on getting the hug, and not on the child guessing correctly. It is amazing how blocking eye contact can make otherwise embarrassing nurturing possible. Although Theraplay stresses the importance of eye contact (and so do we), sometimes eliminating it for a time allows children to get a sample of nurturing which can then be built upon. Also, not being able to see adds challenge and fun.

Blanket Merry-Go-Round

One child sits in the middle of a good sized blanket. The group picks up the edges of the blanket and walks around turning the blanket in a circle **without** lifting the center person off the ground. Sing a song while giving each person a ride. (Orlick, 1982, pg. 46)

Swinging in a Sheet

This is for children either small enough or strong enough for one to actually be picked up in a sheet by the group. It is just like Blanket Merry-Go-Round, except the group very carefully holds the blanket or sheet and lifts the person **slowly** off the ground, swaying him gently for a short time.

Touch Colors

This game is modifiable for varying levels of difficulty, challenge, and cooperation. At its easiest, the group sits in a tight circle. The leader picks a color, saying, "Touch blue," for example. Then she touches something blue **on someone else,** and one-by-one, each person has a turn to touch something blue without others letting go! At the end, everyone should be touching someone else.

With a more sophisticated group, you can all reach for your blue color at the same time — but **no hurts!** Each child can have a chance to pick the next color to touch. For older groups, everyone can touch one color, then hold that color and touch a new color with another part of his body, seeing how many colors you can touch at one time. This last modification has not really been tried with our groups yet, but it does sound like fun! We challenge YOU to try it! (Orlick, 1982, pp. 61, 195)

Guess Who's the Leader?

One child is picked to leave the room. The rest of the group picks a leader. This leader will begin with one movement (clapping hands, patting head, swaying, etc.), but after a few rounds, he will switch to another movement for a few rounds. The leader continues to vary his movements. Meanwhile, the rest of the group must follow the leader's constantly varying movements! Then, the first child is called back into the room, and must guess who the leader is. Naturally, he must carefully watch the children in the group to see who they might be looking at, or which child is the first to change his movement. This really requires the children to work together and to be highly aware of each other.

Paper Patticake

Partners play patticake with both hands clapping the other's hands, but with a piece of construction paper between their hands! They must try not to let the paper fall. It is amazing how cooperative the partners become. This is not an easy game. But the challenge is perfect for older and well established groups. (Orlick, 1982, pg. 52)

People Shapes

The children cooperate to make shapes by lying down on the floor in a pattern. They can start with squares, circles, etc.; then they can try letters, numbers, words, etc. One class made a 1 with one child, a 2 with two children, etc., until the whole class formed numbers and we took a picture. Another class did it by having volunteers to be part of each number, so that each time a number was made, some of the children made the number and others watched, directed, and admired the result. Then they switched places and made the next number. (Orlick, 1978, pg. 12)

Blindfolded Friend Guess

Every group gets caught up in the challenge of this game. Each person (one at a time), including adults, gets blindfolded and must guess—by feeling, smelling, whatever—the person who is picked to sit in front of him. For older children who might peek under a blindfold, have each child's neighbors help to hold a large pillow in front of his face while watching that he should not peek. The kids love it when the adults guess wrong! (Brody, pg. 31)

Over and Over

The children stand behind each other in a line. The first child holds a ball and passes it over his head to the next person and so on down the line. The last person runs to the front of the line with the ball and starts it going over everyone's head again. The group can be challenged to move the group, relay by relay, from one point in the room to another. With more space, this game can be changed to Over and Under, in which kids must alternate passing the ball over their heads and under their legs. (There needs to be more space between the children so they have room to bend.) (Orlick, 1978, pg. 43)

Where's the Lotion?

All members of the group, except for two partners, hide their eyes. One partner puts lotion (or rubs in powder) on the other so that it does not show. The others, one by one and gently, must guess—by smelling, of course—where the lotion or powder was rubbed.

Special Lists

In long-standing groups (year-long), as the ending approaches, each person (including the leader) has a special list made about him that can be taken home as a remembrance. Each group member says something about the person whose turn it is to be "special." The leader writes the comments down, and the lists can be displayed in the room until all are finished. There are different focuses that can be given to the lists you make. One year our lists were example #1. The next year in the same class, we did example #2.

1. What you think is most special about the person.
2. Tell one thing the person does that you do not like, and one thing the person does that you do like.
3. "Bad Day List"—for bad days: Each person says what he does when he is having a bad day. Members of the class can talk about their own behavior, how to be aware of what they or their peers are feeling, more constructive ways to act, or ways to avoid getting someone else's bad day passed on to you. (This is for the oldest and most sophisticated groups.)

Finding Shapes in Another's Hand

Each person must find a shape or letter in the lines on his neighbor's palm. Outline the shape with lotion, or chalk. Show it to the group. Then, of course, you get to rub the lotion into your hand, or share excess lotion with others in the group!

Tug of Peace

Break into small groups of three to five people. Each group gets a long piece of rope. Each group must hold its rope in such a way as to make letters or numbers. These can be held horizontally or vertically. (Orlick, 1978, pg. 15)

Faces or Noises

Everyone has a turn to make the funniest, meanest, etc., face he can or the funniest noise he can. The children often make faces and noises during Theraplay sessions anyway, and turning this natural occurrence into a planned activity invariably brings the children into the adult's structure.

Shaping Twin Statues

Three people from the group are picked. One is the statue shaper, the second is the statue, and the third is the statue's twin. The shaper gets blindfolded. Then the statue person strikes a position. The shaper must feel the statue, and put the third person into the same position as the statue. The shaper is un-blindfolded to see how closely he was able to shape twin statues. (Orlick, 1982, pg. 66)

Cotton Ball Blows

Each person can try blowing a small cotton puff ball off various body parts (elbow, shoulder, knee, shoe!) to other classmates, or try blowing it to the body parts of their peers ("I'm going to blow this to your nose!") These are similar to games you can play with foam balls and crazy foam.

Circle Peas Porridge Hot

This is a harder form of Patticake, so children from six to eight years of age have been challenged by it. In a circle, you alternate clapping your neighbor's hands (as in Patticake) and clapping your own hands once while chanting the song. Since that should be easy, next try it with everyone's eyes closed!

Peas Porridge hot	Some like it hot.
Peas Porridge cold	Some like it cold.
Peas Porridge in the pot	Some like it in the pot
Nine days old.	Nine days old.

Hand Moldings

Bring aluminum foil and a pillow. Lay a piece of foil on top of the pillow. Each person can make an impression of a body part (hands, feet, elbows, chins, knees, etc.) by gently pushing the part into the foil while peers help shape the foil around the part. Gently remove your body— the impression is on the underside of the foil. These can be unique souvenirs of the session or the Theraplay Group. (Jernberg, 1979, pg. 118)

Body Part Pair Walk

Partners must walk around a specified area with different parts of their bodies touching: shoulder-to-shoulder, back-to-back, nose-to-nose, etc. (Orlick, 1978, pg. 35)

Valentine Tear

Partners get a piece of construction paper. Each puts one hand behind his back and holds the paper with the other hand. Together they try to tear the paper into the shape of a heart. (Other shapes can be used for other occasions.) This can be frustrating.

Crazy Foam Sculpture

Each child has a turn to form a part of a sculpture out of crazy foam. When finished, the class can keep the sculpture and see how long it lasts.

Giant Sandal

This is a growing partner game. Start with two children. They get two towels or pieces of construction paper, something they can walk on safely. They each put one foot on one towel and the other foot on the other towel and must walk together without coming off the towels. Real togetherness! If couples can do it—increase to three people together. Also you can vary how the partners walk.

1. Partners face the same direction and walk forward and then backward; they can walk sideways also.
2. Partners face each other and try the same series of walks. (Orlick, 1982, pg. 151)

Mirroring

One partner is the person, the other is the mirror. The person moves slowly (while standing in one place) and the mirror imitates him as simultaneously as possible. The children need to really work together in order to do this well. (Brody, pg. 30)

There is one important caution in choosing this game, however. With children who are not certain as to who they are, not well differentiated from others, mirroring can make them feel "creepy" and fearful of losing their fragile body boundaries. With such children, avoid this activity (Jernberg, personal communication).

Cross-Over Dodgeball

The group divides into teams and stands facing each other. Towels, enough for half of the entire group, are given to various group members on both teams. On cue, people start throwing towels, trying to have them land on people on the other team. When someone is "hit," he must cross-over to the other team. If there is an end to this game, it is when all people are on one side! Otherwise, it is a fun, NON–HURTFUL way to express mock anger. (Orlick, 1978, pg. 47)

Writing with Another's Hand

Have ready large pieces of paper and markers. One person holds the marker and is either blindfolded or closes his eyes. The other person holds the hand that is holding the marker (he cannot hold the marker itself!) and guides the hand to write his own name, or a message, on the paper. Then the blindfold comes off so all can see the message and how well they cooperated to write together. The person blindfolded cannot write what he wants. He must be led by his partner.

Blind Letter on the Back

One child turns his back to the rest of the circle. His neighbor traces a letter, number, or shape on his back with his finger. (Everyone else is watching, of course.) The first child must guess what was traced. This may be difficult for learning-disabled children. Be sure the tracer does not trace so hard that it hurts. But it may be that a timid child traces so gently that the shape cannot be felt, so he must be encouraged, by the "feeler" or the adult, to trace a bit harder.

Connecting Eyes

The group stands in a circle. The children look around until they connect eyes with someone. As two children make eye contact, they exchange places in the circle. Children who tend to avoid eye contact cannot avoid it in this game! (Orlick, 1982, pg. 87)

Nose to Nose

The group watches as one child closes his eyes and tries to connect his nose with the nose of his neighbor who is watching but remains still. If necessary, the child who can see can make noises (sighing, clicking) to help the first child find his way. This is another good way to promote closeness with older children. (Orlick, 1982, pg. 90)

Dots

This is a very challenging, and verbal, game. A large paper is mounted on the wall. One child is blindfolded and a classmate marks a dot somewhere on the paper with a marker. The blindfolded child is given a marker of a different color, and is helped to place his marker on the paper. The class takes turns in a joint effort to give verbal directions that the blindfolded child must follow to lead him to the dot.

The directions can be simple (up, down, sideways) or more sophisticated (left, right; east, west) depending on the level of the group. This requires the children to take fair turns, respond to the directions of others, and to modify misinterpreted messages. To make this more challenging, an adult can keep a score of the number of directions needed to get to the dot, as incentive for developing more responsiveness and involvement.

Non-Verbal Birthday Lineup

Without talking, the children must line up in order of age — or whose birthday comes first. (Orlick, 1978, pg. 48)

Dr. Tangle

Two people (one adult if necessary) leave the room or go to a far corner. The rest of the group holds hands in a circle and then twists itself into a tangle. The first two people come back and must gently untangle the group without breaking them apart. (Orlick, 1978, pg. 39)

Aura or Vibes!

Two people stand facing each other at arm's length and touch finger tips. They close their eyes or are blindfolded. Then they both take three steps backward and turn around three times (all with help from the group). Then the two people must try to find each other again by sensing their "aura" and once more touching finger tips. This can be as interesting a game to do as to watch! Try doing this with the entire group at one time. (Fluegelman, 1976, pg. 37)

SUCCESSFUL LARGE GROUP ACTIVITIES

Big Snake

The children get into a crawling position and hold onto the ankles of the child in front of them. (They can start out in pairs and grow bigger and bigger until they make a giant snake.) Then they try to move around the designated area in one piece — they can try moving backward, try "going to sleep"—anything that snakes do. **Keeping together** is the real task. (Orlick, 1978, pg. 14)

Detective

Pass around a large hand-held magnifying glass. Look at each other's beautiful eyes, beautiful noses, etc. Admire! This develops great eye contact. (DaCosse)

Eskimo

Pretend to be Eskimos with your bodies all bundled up except for your noses. Hug each other by passing an Eskimo kiss: rubbing noses together! (DaCosse)

Butterfly Kisses

Set the scene by talking about butterfly wings. Then use your eyelashes to kiss or flutter against the next person's cheek. In my class, "kissing" was very popular and the children came up with a lot of their own kinds of kisses. We played cheek kissing, chin kissing, and one that really tested their skill at being gentle—forehead kissing! (DaCosse)

Bunny Tails

Hold up a large cotton ball. Call it a bunny's tail and explain that it is for gently tickling a friend's chin. As each person leans over to the next person's chin, he says, "Chinny-chin-chin." You are welcome to say anything you like!! (DaCosse)

I See Somebody Special

This can be done two different ways, depending on the season. Take a hand mirror and drape a scarf over it, concealing the mirror. Tell the group that each of them will peek under the scarf and will see "someone **very special.**" Tell them to look for two beautiful eyes, a soft squishy nose and a big wonderful smile, but not to tell anyone who it is. Make them promise not to tell! This builds the excitement.

The second version which really was fun, was putting a small round compact mirror inside a plastic pantihose egg. Say that you have a special person inside, and that each child should take the top off, look inside, and look real close at the "special person's" eyes, etc. Again, they must not tell anyone who is in the egg! (DaCosse)

Tongue Curls

Some people can curl their tongues and others cannot. It's all in the genes. Whether or not you can, you can always find a child who can. Go around the circle finding those that can and those who cannot. The fun is sticking out your tongue and trying. When you find those that can, enjoy the discovery of their "specialness." (DaCosse)

Face Painting

You need a soft, dry paint brush and an empty egg carton. If you have a large group, use two sets and start at both ends of the circle. You explain that this is a magical brush and inside are magical colors. There is a magical green, magical blue, etc. You dip into a magic color and paint the face of the child next to you. I called out the colors I was using, wiped the paint off the sides of the brush, and painted the child, stressing that I was taking care to be very gentle. When you are through, make sure the child shows his face to the group. His facial expression is priceless—so is this work of art. (DaCosse)

Funny Faces

This starts out with the whole group imitating a silly face that **you** make. Then as the group gets better at it, you can call out a feeling, such as an angry face, and try to pass that around the circle. Sometimes, you are laughing too hard to maintain the face. That's OK—you're having fun! (DaCosse)

Pretzeling

Don't ask where this one came from, but it is a favorite. Sit in a circle and put your legs out in front of you. Do some form of "pretzeling," count to three, then "unpretzel." To pretzel, you cross your legs, cross your arms, criss-cross arms with someone else's arms, cross legs with a neighbor, cross arms with another neighbor, or criss-cross your arms over your head. There are many variations!! (DaCosse)

Make a Round Circle—Color it Purple

This activity is based on a family tradition and was used with a baby to get it to quiet down and go to sleep, but it adapts well to Theraplay Groups. One child is either blindfolded, closes his eyes, or turns his back so he cannot see. You take your finger and pick a part of the body such as his nose or cheek. You trace a circle on that body part with your finger, saying, "Make a round circle, color it purple. S.O.M.E.B.O.D.Y poke!" (Stretching out the word "somebody.") Then the person who has been poked has to guess who did the poking. (DaCosse)

Is it Huggable?

Pass around any stuffed animal, doll, or another child. Slowly draw that animal, doll, or child close to you and slowly envelop it into a hug. Is it huggable? You bet! (DaCosse)

Telephone Line

If broken toys are a common occurrence in your classroom, create imaginary ones! For this game, pass an **imaginary** telephone by talking into your baby finger and thumb. Say the name of the person next to you: "Tommy, it's for you." Usually all you will hear is silence as the child is "listening" to the phone. The fun is if the children remember to say "It's for you," and the anticipatory wait to see what that person might say. (DaCosse)

Musical Instruments

Using different parts of the body, you play music. Use your arms to play an imaginary violin, your legs to play a guitar, slap your knees or thighs for drums, etc. Then you can gently "play" on someone else. The piano is easy to "play" on your neighbor's leg or arm or back. Drums can be a bit of a challenge, but they usually are a favorite. (DaCosse)

Acknowledgment

Fourteen specified games from *The Cooperative Sports and Games Book* by Terry Orlick. Copyright © 1978 by Terry Orlick. Reprinted by permission of Pantheon Books, a Division of Random House, Inc.

Twelve specified games from *The Second Cooperative Sports and Games Book* by Terry Orlick. Copyright © 1982 by Terry Orlick. Reprinted by permission of Pantheon Books, a Division of Random House, Inc.

Appendix 1

THE TRAINING EXPERIENCE

During the training workshops, our trainees told us about their experiences in "unlearning" being a teacher and learning the Theraplay approach. They also had delightful stories about how their children were responding to these new groups. The following are their stories.

Although all the trainees either had heard about Theraplay from their colleagues, or had participated in a Theraplay Group in their classroom, learning to create the Theraplay atmosphere and being "Theraplayish" did not always come easily. Mary Alice DaCosse described her experience:

"Don't get the idea I jumped right in and bubbled over with enthusiasm. Far from it. I was exhausted and just a little afraid. This was a whole new language. Theraplay had a new set of rules, and being a Theraplay Group leader was a whole new role to add to what I already felt was an extensive repertoire. But I did it anyway.

"Conducting Theraplay groups was like student teaching all over again. Instead of a supervising teacher watching over me in the classroom, I had a video camera recording the sessions. As a Theraplay Group leader, I had to learn a new language and try to discard the dictatorial ways of a teacher. I had a new set of rules, a new environment, and a new format."

Most of the trainees had difficulty with two complementary tasks: giving up their teacherish, unfun way of structuring, and having pure fun. They automatically would prepare the group for what they were going to do in the session by giving the name of the game ("Now we're going to play Partner Stand Ups."), and by going into a narrative of how the game would be played. In watching their videotapes, they became aware of how routine and predictable they sounded, and how boring it was for even them— let alone their children—to listen to their often too long explanation of how to play the game. They began to laugh when they heard themselves announce the name of each game, realizing that this was usually totally unnecessary. They began to realize that, if they were ever going to create **fun** in their groups, they would have to just jump in and **DO!**

And they began to try. They jumped in quicker. But, while they never seemed to have difficulty keeping structure in their group, they did continue to have trouble with having fun **themselves.** We spent a good part of one training session talking about what having fun meant. They realized they would need to feel comfortable "being silly" and "being childish," and being this way **in front of their children.** For some, this was easier to do than it was for others.

It also seemed that the two regular education teachers had less trouble having fun themselves in their groups than the special education teachers with smaller classes. This may have been because, in the larger classes, the children were more able to play a game together for an extended period of time and generate their own fun, as well as their own structure, allowing the teacher to relax and enjoy her class's pleasure.

After the second workshop session, the trainees were asked to lead a brief Theraplay Group with their class, consisting of only getting-to-know-you activities. At the next session, they were asked to add structuring activities to their Group sessions.

At this point, regardless of how hard or easy it was for the teacher to achieve a Theraplay approach to her group, the trainees began coming to the workshops with stories about how their classes were already responding. They noticed that their withdrawn children were participating, and their quiet children were verbalizing. On videotapes, we saw increased sharing, cooperation, and positive interacting that the teachers reported carried over into other parts of the school day. The teachers wondered if they were imagining things, but they felt that their classes were calmer. It couldn't possibly be the Group, could it? How could it affect their classes so quickly? It is indeed surprising, but it is true, that Theraplay can have an immediate effect on a child or on a group of children.

The kindergarten and first grade classes took to the Theraplay Groups like ducks to water. They jumped right in and were ready for fun. And the children quickly generalized their experience in the groups. Karen McCabe related with delight the following story:

Her class was walking through the hall of the school. She turned around when she heard one child tell a classmate, who was drifting out of the line, to "stick together." And then it generalized further: her children began telling children in other classes that **they** should stick together, too!

All the teachers found that their children were highly responsive to the nurturing provided in the group. In this case, it was the regular education teachers who were most surprised at how much nurturing their children seemed to need, now that they had made it available and acceptable. To all the children in every group, the nurturing experiences became important and very meaningful. Children began to notice and become concerned about the discomfort of others, and this generalized to other parts of the school day. They reminded the teacher if she forgot to give a child his turn, or forgot to take her own turn! Lisa Tatar came up with the concept of an "outside hurt" and an "inside hurt," allowing children who did not have an obvious hurt to get nurtured for a private reason.

And the trainees themselves began to generalize what they were learning from the Theraplay approach and apply it with children who were resisting schoolwork. They found, still to their surprise, that when they did so, the children became more willing to learn. For example, one teacher simply put a resistive child on her lap and found that his anxiety decreased and he was able to complete his work with no more encouragement than the lap!

However, as their children continued to get, and some began to demand, more and more nurturing, some teachers asked a new question of us. They were trying to stop giving nurturing in their group. How could they get away from nurturing now that their children had come to expect it? We wondered what had scared these teachers away from nurturing when it was clear that their children needed it. What were they afraid of? It turned out that their worst fear was that a child's mother might come to pick him up from school, and that the child would not want to leave!

As the trainees became more familiar and comfortable with the Theraplay atmosphere and balancing various types of activities, they began to ask how they could determine what particular Theraplay message(s) an individual child might need. We discussed three ways of getting information that would help them.

1. Observing the child's behavior with others: Did he innocently hurt other children? Was he unable to assert or express his needs? Was he always bossing others?
2. Seeing the child with his parent(s): Did they ignore his attempts to

communicate? Were they too lenient (unstructuring) or too punitive or rough? Did they expect to hear only negative things about
their child? Were they able to be appropriately positive and responsive to him?

3. Learning about the child's and family's history while he was growing up: surgeries, moving, caretakers, family/marital problems,
sibling problems, pregnancy or birth problems.

The answers to these questions could signal to the Theraplay Group
leader that the child needs more nurturing or more structuring, for
example, or that he is a "little adult," etc.

One classes' progress was of particular surprise and delight to us.
Susan Noble Pelafas continued leading her group throughout the final
year of supervision that qualified her as a Theraplay Child Group
Specialist. She was able to monitor changes in her children across one
calendar year of having a Theraplay Group. What is significant is that
hers was a class of severely autistic and developmentally delayed children,
a class we would have previously thought unable to benefit from such a
group approach.

In the first session of the introductory workshop, all the trainees were
asked to write group goals for their Theraplay Groups. Susan wrote that
she hoped that there would be an increase in appropriate play interaction among her children, and that they would become more aware of
each other and of those around them. When we saw her goals, we
privately thought, "These children are autistic. They will never achieve
these goals." But were we in for a surprise!

Her withdrawn, self-stimulating children who did not interact with
others—some of whom even seemed to be unaware that others existed—
began to change. Susan began to see an increase in their awareness of
each other even before our workshops were over. Across the next school
year, she observed further changes she never would have predicted.

Not only were the children more aware of each other, but also they
became aware of other people who happened to come into their room.
Previously, if someone new had come in, they seemed oblivious, going
on with their own isolating activity. Now, they alerted, realizing there
was a new presence in the room.

They began to spontaneously share play objects and food when before,
they could share nothing. One child spontaneously fed another a cookie!

The children became willing to touch one another, when before they would shrink away from any touch, like most autistic children. When they had gone for walks before, they had walked alone, separately, unconnected to one another. Now they **all** (!) held hands and walked **as a group.** (We are amazed each time we think of this.)

During water play, one child took her turn, then went to her peer who was standing close by, interested, but unable to initiate his own water play. She pushed him to the water, let him take a turn, then pushed him back, and took her turn. Again, she pushed him to the water for a turn, repeating this sharing, turn-taking process. This from a girl who had been totally demanding, possessive, and teasing of others! This demonstrates the development she had made from the stage of egocentric infant to the stage of sharing child.

Another child, previously in her own world unless physically touched and face-to-face with another insistent presence, now helped her peers. She watched others, and when they were having problems, she went over and did it for them!

The boy in the group, previously pretty much of a blob, had developed a "little personality." He became more defiant (the "no" stage of childhood). When told to stop doing something, he did it again, sometimes yelling, "No!" Sue now described him as "bubbly." He even got excited about things!

Now, when one child had tantrums, another would start to cry. Whereas before, such tantrums could occur and no other child seemed aware of what was happening, now this child would have to be removed from the room because the crying of her "friend" **upset her**!

Trips now became events for the children. Before, they had never shown any change in emotion when it was time to take a walk outside or go on the bus to a new place. Now they showed signs of anticipation when getting ready for an outing.

Sue reported one more significant detail. There was now much better eye contact. These children who had actively avoided making eye contact, now began to **look** at adults and to **look** at their classmates.

This is not to say that these children were no longer autistic or severely delayed. While it may sound on paper like they made a 360 degree change, what we have related were incidents and interactions among still autistic children. What was exciting about this for both Susan and ourselves, is that these were **new, spontaneous,** and **interactive** behaviors that seemed to flow out of the Theraplay Group experience. Some, like feeding each other, clearly seemed to come from the children's having participated in this type of activity during the group. These were not impersonal skills, such as learning to eat with a spoon, but interpersonal achievements. The children had become more conscious of, and interested in interacting with, **other people.**

For those of you who work with such severely involved children, they will need continual experiences such as Theraplay and Theraplay Groups in order to maintain such growth and interactions. Teachers and therapists have found that, without constant stimulation and insistent involvement, autistic children cannot sustain an interest in the world and people. They will quickly return to isolated play.

Appendix 2

PERMISSION FORMS FOR VIDEOTAPING

Parental permission must be given in order to videotape others. The following are the forms we developed for the needs of our trainees. They give examples of what you may want to include in your forms. You can use these forms as they are, if they meet your needs.

Form I introduces the Theraplay Group itself, so that the parents are prepared for what is happening at school and the experiences that their child may talk about at home. It is helpful for them to know that crazy foam, powder, or marker may appear on their child's clothes or hands, and that they all will wash out. This will avoid the phone calls that put you on the defensive after your Theraplay Group has started. If you want to request that girls wear jeans/pants on Theraplay Group day, this is the place to do it.

You may want to ask whether the child has any food allergies, so that you will be aware of this when choosing the treat for the group.

Some of you may want parent permission for each child to participate in the Theraplay Group itself, which you can include in this form, Form II, or in a separate form.

Form I also explains the reason for videotaping the group.

Form II is the permission for videotaping. Included are the arrangements one can make in the taping situation so that parents concerned with their child's privacy will still be comfortable and allow him to participate in a group that is being videotaped. Also listed are the possible situations in which you may want to show the tapes. Some parents may agree to some of these situations but not to others.

Form III is for parents who do not give permission for their child to participate in videotaping that will be shown only to the group trainer and the teacher. If you receive this response to your request for permission by even one parent, it will put you at a disadvantage if you are seeking training, supervision, or for your own self-monitoring. Your

179

choices will either be to not do the group, to eliminate that child from the group, or to not videotape. None of these choices are good.

Form III asks the parent for permission for **only you** to view the videotapes. Some parents may even want you to erase the tapes when you are finished with them. Although this will limit the usefulness of the tapes to you, you must understand that the parents are protecting their child and themselves from unwanted exposure. You must respect this. If the parents will allow **only you** to view the tapes, it will ensure that you get the feedback that you need to lead an effective group.

If you do not get permission from a parent to videotape a child, we would recommend going ahead with your group, but allocate time to write notes soon afterward describing what happened. Be sure to have conferred with your co-leader(s), so that you have different perspectives on what the children did, and what you did. (Or they can write their own notes separately and give them to you.) These can also be used for training in lieu of videotapes.

FORM I

Dear Parents,

We will be starting a new activity in our classroom on _____.
Once a week, we will have a Theraplay Group with the entire class. This
group will be geared toward improving your child's ability to socialize
and communicate with other children and adults. We will be working on
the following goals:

The emphasis in Theraplay is to engage children in play activities
that will help them to better get along with one another. During the
sessions we will participate in enjoyable, cooperative activities together.
We will be sitting on mats or on a rug on the floor, so have your child
dress comfortably on Group Day. Materials that we use in these activities
are lotion, powder, water-color markers, and crazy foam. Should they get
on your child's clothes, they will wash out in the laundry. We often share
treats in our group (pretzels or crackers).

We would like to be able to videotape our group from time to time.
The purposes of videotaping would be twofold:

1. I am participating in a training program to learn to lead this
   Theraplay Group. Watching videotapes of our group will help me
   in my training.
2. These videotapes will allow me to assess your child's progress in
   the goals listed above.

Since we need your permission to videotape, please sign the attached
permission form and return it to school by _____.

If you have any questions about this group, please call me at _____.

Thank you,

FORM II
PERMISSION FOR VIDEOTAPING

I give my permission for my child to be videotaped during Theraplay Group sessions during the _____ school year. I understand that these videotapes will be used only for professional, non-commercial purposes.

Please cross out and initial any uses of the videotapes for which you DO NOT give permission:

1. Videotaping with my child shown as part of the group.   _____
2. Videotaping with my child positioned out of camera range.   _____
3. Videotapes can be viewed by professionals being trained in
   Theraplay Groups.   _____
4. Videotapes can be viewed by parent groups.   _____
5. Videotapes can be viewed by agency staff participating in the
   Theraplay training program.   _____
6. Videotapes can be viewed by my child's teacher and Theraplay
   Group trainer(s).   _____

Parent's signature: _____

Name of student: _____

Date: _____

School: _____

FORM III

Dear _____,

I understand that you do not want your child to participate in videotaping that will be shown to others. I respect your wish. However, I would like to be able to view the videotapes. Let me explain why it is important that I can do this.

During a Theraplay Group, many things may occur between the children themselves and between children and teachers, and these may occur very quickly. The best method of reviewing what has happened in the group is by watching a videotape of the session.

Also, as I have explained before, videotapes will show if your child has improved in the goals we have set for him/her. In academic subjects, we can use tests to show improvement. In social and communication skills, videotaping is the best way to show improvement.

Therefore, I ask you to give permission for **only myself** to view the videotapes of your child's Theraplay Group. I will then be able to assess the group, and monitor your child's progress. Your child, as well as the entire class, will benefit from this process.

Please fill out the permission form below and return it to school with your child. Thank you for your cooperation.

Sincerely,

I give permission for my child to be videotaped during Theraplay Group sessions during the _____ school year. These videotapes will be viewed only by my child's teacher.

Parent's signature: _____

Name of student: _____

Date: _____

School: _____

REFERENCES

Brody, Viola, Fenderson, Caroline and Stephenson, Susan, "Sourcebook for Finding Your Way to Helping Young Children Through Developmental Play," 1015 10th Avenue North, St. Petersburg, FL: Pupil Personnel Services Demonstration Project, 1976.

DesLauriers, A. M., and Carlson, C., *Your Child Is Asleep: Early Infantile Autism,* Homewood, IL: Dorsey, 1969.

DesLauriers, Austin M., *The Experience of Reality in Childhood Schizophrenia,* New York: International Universities Press, 1962.

Fluegelman, Andrew, *The New Games Book,* Garden City: Doubleday, 1976.

Golden, Bernard R., "Theraplay: Facilitating Healthy Narcissism," *Theraplay Newsletter,* Fall, 1983.

Jernberg, Ann M., *Theraplay,* San Francisco: Jossey-Bass, 1979.

Orlick, Terry, *The Cooperative Sports and Games Book,* New York: Pantheon, 1978.

Orlick, Terry, *The Second Cooperative Sports and Games Book,* New York: Pantheon, 1982.

Rubin, Phyllis, "Teaching Pragmatics in Special Education Classes Using Group Theraplay", videotape presented at the American Speech-Language-Hearing Association Convention, 1984.

Rubin, Phyllis, and Tregay, Jeanine, "The Use of Group Theraplay in the Special Education Classroom," presented at the Illinois Council for Exceptional Children Convention, 1984.

Rubin, P., and Tregay, J., "Developing Social Skills Using Theraplay Groups," presented at the Chicago Association for the Education of Young Children Convention, 1986.

Rubin, P., Tregay, J., and Mirabito, Diane, "Group Theraplay in the Special Education Classroom," presented at the National Association of School Social Workers Convention, 1985.

INDEX OF THERAPLAY ACTIVITIES

187

Available this Fall

EVALUATION AND EDUCATIONAL PROGRAMMING OF STUDENTS WITH DEAFBLINDNESS AND SEVERE DISABILITIES
Sensorimotor State (2nd Ed.)

To be published 2001, 294 pages
Caroll J. Jones
Price not yet available, paper

DEVELOPING AND IMPLE-MENTING IDEA-IEPs
An Individualized Education Program (IEP) Handbook for Meeting Individuals with Disabilities Education Act (IDEA) Requirements

Published 2001, 222 pages
Edward Burns

CURRICULUM DEVELOPMENT FOR STUDENTS WITH MILD DISABILITIES
Academic and Social Skills for Inclusion IEPs

Published 2000, 258 pages
Carroll J. Jones
$34.95, spiral (paper)

AUTISM AND POST-TRAUMATIC STRESS DISORDER
Ending Autistic Fixation

Published 2000, 136 pages
Kenneth Lenchitz
$36.95, cloth
$19.95, paper (displayed)

PARENTAL INVOLVEMENT
A Practical Guide for Collaboration and Teamwork for Students with Disabilities

Published 2000, 202 pages
George Taylor
$39.95, hard
$26.95, paper

Programmed Therapy FOR STUTTERING in Children and Adults (2nd Ed.)

Published 2000, 360 pages
Bruce P. Ryan
$79.95, hard
$54.95, paper

THE THINKING SKILLS WORKBOOK
A Cognitive Skills Remediation Manual for Adults (3rd Ed.)

Published 2000, 284 pages
Lynn Tondat-Ruggeri, Mary Languirand & John L. Caruso
$39.95, spiral (paper)

DISABILITY AWARENESS IN THE CLASSROOM
A Resource Tool for Teachers and Students

Published 1999, 230 pages
Lorie Levison & Isabelle St. Onge
$48.95 spiral (paper)

DEAFNESS AND VISION DISORDERS
Anatomy and Physiology, Assessment Procedures, Ocular Anomalies, and Educational Implications

Published 1999, 520 pages
Donald D. Johnson
$77.95, cloth

CHILDREN WITH SPECIAL NEEDS
A Resource Guide for Parents, Educators, Social Workers, and Other Care-givers

Published 1999, 234 pages
Karen L. Lunglu
$51.95, cloth
$38.95, paper (displayed)

SOMETHING'S WRONG WITH MY CHILD!
A Valuable Resource in Helping Parents and Professionals to Better Understand Themselves in Dealing with the Emotionally Charged Subject of Children with Disabilities (2nd Ed.)

Published 1998, 234 pages
Harriet Wallace Rose
$48.95, cloth
$35.95, paper (displayed)

BRIDGING THE FAMILY-PROFESSIONAL GAP
Facilitating Interdisciplinary Services for Children With Disabilities

Published 1999, 300 pages
Billy T. Ogletree, Martin A. Fischer & Jane B. Schulz
$51.95, cloth
$38.95, paper (displayed)

I CAN'T HEAR YOU IN THE DARK
How to Learn and Teach Lipreading

Published 1998, 226 pages
Betty Woerner Carter
$36.95, spiral (paper)